THE RAW TRUTH TO SUCCESS IN REAL ESTATE

"A true American success story: Engelo lands in the Land of Opportunity with nothing more than an incredible drive and vision for his future. Through the years he has built one of the premier turnkey brands in the U.S. His passion for his product and clients is self-evident, and his success is simply an American success story!"

— Jay Hinrichs,
Real Estate Developer and Broker

"The Dingo's book is the swift kick in the arse new investors need to get focused and cut through the nonsense they are bombarded with every time they search 'how to get started in real estate' and end up accidentally selling an arm and a leg to learn something that they could have figured out on their own had they just picked up this book first. Don't be a Johnny Talker, be a Johnny Walker and add this book to your real estate education arsenal."

— Justin Stamper,
Host of *Zombie House Flipping* on A&E

"If you're looking for a motivating feel-good book, this isn't your book. Engelo isn't your author, and frankly, real estate isn't your industry. However, if you're looking to hear things from the perspective of a no-bull$#@% entrepreneur who's walked the walk, along with talking the talk, then I recommend you give this thing a read. Plus, I've had the guy do a commercial on my show with no freaking pants on … so there's that."

— James Wise,
CEO, Holton-WiscTV

THE
RAW TRUTH
TO SUCCESS IN REAL ESTATE

ENGELO RUMORA

NEW YORK

LONDON • NASHVILLE • MELBOURNE • VANCOUVER

The Raw Truth to Success in Real Estate

Published in New York, New York, by Morgan James Publishing. Morgan James is a trademark of Morgan James, LLC. www.MorganJamesPublishing.com

ISBN 9781631950896 paperback
ISBN 9781631950902 eBook
ISBN 9781631951671 audiobook
Library of Congress Control Number: 2020904404

Cover Design by:
Engelo Rumora

Interior Design by:
Christopher Kirk
www.GFSstudio.com

Morgan James is a proud partner of Habitat for Humanity Peninsula and Greater Williamsburg. Partners in building since 2006.

Get involved today! Visit
MorganJamesPublishing.com/giving-back

For Milka

My thoughts often wander to you standing on the balcony waiting for me to run past. I wish I could talk to you now that I'm a grown man. I'm looking forward to seeing you again one day.

"Fight for what you believe in. Only drop your guns when you are wrong, and then pick them straight up again."
— Drunk man at back-alley noodle bar,
Sydney, Australia, circa 2011

TABLE OF CONTENTS

FOREWORD
(OR MAYBE MINE IS 'BACKWARD')

OK, mates: If someone doesn't sue the bejesus out of me for the content within this book, I'll consider it a success. I didn't mention any names so I should be OK.

I couldn't even get anyone to write a Foreword.

Oh, to hell with it…

Flip the page and read my Preface already!

PREFACE

Let's just put this out there right now: You're probably either going to love what I have to say in this book, or you're going to hate it.

You're going to love me—or hate me.

That's just the way it is. I don't do "diplomacy" or "political correctness." It's not the message; it's because of the way I deliver the message. I call things as I see them. I don't beat around the bush. I tell it like it is.

Why? Because life is just too freaking short! And it won't do me—or you—any good to waste time worrying about whether I'm going to offend you or hurt your feelings with what I have to say when the stakes are so high. Plus, if words like "butt" or "pimp" or even the initials "B.S." throw you off, you need to wake up. In a world of hate and lies, a few mild swear words or epithets are the least you will endure. (See? I've already started offending you!)

I hope you're not looking for a thesis on real estate investing written by Dr. Ph.D. Jerko. My advice goes against the grain in the most unsophisticated and unorthodox way you have ever witnessed.

I mean, look—why did you pick up this book, anyway? I'll wager that your story goes something like this (more or less):

You have a vision of how you want to live—and enjoy—your life but slogging your way through that 9-to-5 job just isn't cutting it. You're not making any financial headway, and you're tired—so very tired—of waiting for your proverbial "ship to come in."

Somewhere along the way you've heard how powerful real estate investing can be as a wealth builder. Maybe a family member, friend or neighbor is a real estate investor. Or maybe you've been hypnotized by a late-night-TV guru or gotten sucked up into the fake drama of one of those fix-and-flip shows on HGTV.

No matter how you came to this realization, you're here now and you want a piece of the action. So, congratulations, and welcome to the wonderful world of real estate investing! But if you think the road ahead is going to be easy, you are sadly mistaken, my mate.

If you continue to believe that—and you continue to shove every spare dollar into some "get-rich-quick" program (almost 99% of them are B.S., as the information is available for FREE online)—you are going to be wasting both your money and your precious time. And when time is gone, you can never, ever, ever get it back again.

Wouldn't you rather be working hard to actually produce the money that will allow you the freedom to live life on your own terms?

Then, listen—*now*—to what I'm telling you!

Those gurus don't care how long it takes you to go through their courses before they christen you "ready" to make your first deal; the longer, the better, as far as they're concerned. Because the more time you spend "learning" from them just means more money in their pockets. But here's the kicker: Some of them have never invested a dime of their own in a real estate deal! What the hell, right?

On the other hand, what I promise you in the following pages is an unfiltered look at real estate investing from somebody who's been in the trenches—somebody who's still in the trenches with you, as a matter of fact—and who knows what it takes to succeed. (Get your guns ready.)

I've stumbled and fallen more than a few times—and that's to your benefit, so that, now, maybe you won't have to make the same mistakes. You, too, can learn to achieve wealth through real estate investing like I have, but your road can be just a little smoother and get you to your ultimate goal just a little bit sooner.

Listen, mates, my purpose here is not to write a best seller that's going to make millions. Or to "spruik" you on to some B.S. mastermind course, etc. ... yuck! I'm doing just fine as a real estate investor, thank you very much! Here's the truth: I'd much rather have the honor of having written the worst-selling book of all time (Is there even such a list?)—as long as my message can change even just one person's life for the better. *That* would mean success to me.

This book is not about making you guys like me, but rather about sharing my hard-earned knowledge and beliefs in a passionate, straightforward—OK, yeah, maybe even rude—way. It's just *The Raw Truth*!

Why should you listen to me? Believe me, mates, as you will witness throughout this book, I've seen it all!

I've worked very hard for a dream and reached it. I've also fallen to the lowest of lows and had to dig deep to find the will to come back. (Don't you dare start thinking "rags to riches." Not my point.) I've started with nothing and achieved success, then lost my accumulated wealth through both my own arrogance and through trusting the wrong people and taking bad advice.

I'm not the first real estate investor to do that, but if I can help it, *you* won't be among this group.

So, yes, I have a freaking awesome message to share so you can avoid some of those same roadblocks, pitfalls and viper dens with greasy, slimy, snake-oil-selling gurus that I have experienced firsthand. And I'm going to shout it from the rooftops at the top of my lungs!

Be politically correct? Not on your life!! That's just another editing time-waster, and we've got lots of ground to cover.

My words are meant to inspire you—and frankly to kick your butt really, really hard—so you are motivated to take action! Because that's the only way you are going to be successful, whether in real estate or in life. I've seen way too many people who "talk the talk" but don't "walk the walk." Don't be like them.

Be forewarned: I write like I talk—and for people who've met me or heard me speak, they know what that means! (There's a reason this book is called *The Raw Truth*.)

Real estate investing is not for sissies. It's hard work—literally blood, sweat and tears—for all the men and women who are truly committed to making smart, profitable deals the right way.

If you're not willing to work hard, then do us a favor and put this book down. Feel free to move on to the "animal mating" or "gardening" section of your local bookstore.

You've got to have passion and commitment, sure. But you also need an edge.

Here's the edge I promise and which I readily share: The benefit of the know-how and skills that I've gained by making plenty of mistakes and losing lots of money (I'm talking millions…) on my way to learning what real estate investing is all about.

I've also made millions investing in real estate, but the reason I'm writing this book is to pay it forward: To use both my knowledge and my wealth to help you and others like you. I've made mistakes so you don't have to. Or, at least so your stumbles and falls aren't as dramatic or near-catastrophic as mine have been.

Despite those ups and downs, I have always believed real estate investing is the best way to build wealth so you can stop just dreaming about how cool your life can be and actually start living that life. But you've got to know how to do it. And do it right.

So, what do I get in return? Aha! That's the best part: Karma (a suffocating curse if you do wrong and the most seductive, luscious and amazing thing ever if you do right). The more you give, the more you will get, so I'm giving this book to you—so make sure to send some good karma back my way.

In the following pages you will find stuff that I live and breathe every second of every day. These are principles and ideas that shape every aspect of my life. And they work. So, yeah, I'm pumped. I'm excited, and I hope that you are, also.

This is all to say, hang on for one wild ride in the chapters ahead. I'm going to hit you smack dead-center in the face with something the other guys never share: The truth. *The Raw Truth!* Nothing sugar-coated. Just to-the-point, practical, simple content designed to help you succeed and prosper. My pants are coming off in this "be-all and tell-all" thriller of a book.

Think you can handle that?

Then let's go! I promise you won't be disappointed.

P.S.—If you don't find a single piece of useful content, email me at engelo@engelorumora.com and I'll refund you the money. (Ingrates…)

> *"Stop being a Johnny Talker.*
> *Be a Johnny Walker and make it Blue, no ice."*
> — Engelo Rumora

Chapter 1

DON'T BE A LAZY A-HOLE

I've been called a lot of things in my life: Loud. Demanding. Obnoxious. Brash. Pompous. Overbearing. A-hole…

Yeah, I've been called that last one a lot (haha). So many times, in fact, that I've lost count. But I have never … *ever* … ***ever*** been called a *lazy* a-hole.

So why am I starting out this book with a chapter called "Don't Be a Lazy A-hole? Sounds like I'm calling out almost everybody, doesn't it? You bet, I am!

Are you offended yet? Or mad?

"Who the hell does this guy think he is, calling me a lazy a-hole?" I know you're thinking that. And that's good. Because I want you to be mad. Mad enough to prove that I'm wrong in saying that.

I want you to get up off your lazy backside and take action! Because that is the key to success in whatever you do in life. Period.

If there's a singular point to this opening chapter (or the entire book, for that matter), it's that nothing comes easy. You have to put hard work into everything, whether in business or in life. You've got to hustle your tail off if you want to succeed!

"But, Engelo; what about talent? What about opportunity? What about a college degree? Don't they count for something?"

Well, of course those things count, but nowhere near as much as hard work.

Some people *are* "born with" a natural ability to excel at this thing or that. But do they always put their talent to use?

Opportunity *does* knock. But how many people hear it? And even if you do recognize it, what then? Will you answer the knock on the door? Will you do anything with the opportunity?

The point, mates, is this: If you want something, you have to work hard. Very hard. Excruciatingly hard. You have to want to succeed at that goal so much that you are willing to sacrifice anything—and everything—to get there. I know, because I have done it. And I continue to do it every day.

People don't succeed just because they might have some particular knowledge. Likewise, people don't fail just because they don't have that knowledge—yet. What do I mean by that? I mean that you can't sit back waiting for things to be handed to you. You have to work for them. And I also mean that just because you may not be the greatest at something right now, that doesn't mean you can't be. Afraid you won't measure up? Get over it, get off your butt and get to work!

Don't be one of those lazy a-holes who are sitting back waiting for something to be handed to them, or who are convinced they aren't talented/smart enough so they don't even get up to try. The world doesn't owe you a favor.

Guess what? I don't have a bit of sympathy for either one of those types of people.

When you put your mind and efforts to it, you can overcome anything. I'm living proof. I've always said that "If I can do it, so can you."

I'll be the first to tell you I'm not the smartest guy in the world. I mean, I quit school at age 14 so I could pursue my dream of being a professional soccer player. (A goal that I did achieve, by the way.) But in the course of doing that, I didn't get the same amount of "book learning" as other kids my age who went on to finish high school, and then college and maybe then some more: masters and other "voo-doo-economics" stuff.

I don't read fast. I read really—and I mean R E A L L Y—slowly. I can't type fast, since I use the two-finger, "hunt-and-peck" method. So it takes me forever to write something, even though my brain is going a million miles an hour. (I started writing this book when I was 2 years old…)

So, yeah, I was at a disadvantage from day one in every way you look at it. People have been putting me down my whole life.

First, it was, "Engelo, you don't have the lung capacity. You can't run like all of us can. You're too slow. You're never going to make it in soccer."

Then people were telling me, "Engelo, you've got no high school diploma. You can't write. You can't read. You can't type. How can you be successful in business?"

But I didn't listen to them. I didn't quit before I got started. I wasn't sitting back on my lazy backside feeling sorry for myself. Instead, I got up and I took action. I went forward against all odds.

Ultimately, what differentiates me from so many other people and how I have found success in soccer and in business comes down to one simple thing: Hard work.

Here is my guiding philosophy: *I am willing to do today what others won't so that I can live tomorrow like others can't.*

What about you? How hard do you work and how much do you sacrifice?

You see, Comfortable Chris or Cassy, I wake up before everyone, I go to sleep after everyone. I work harder, and I work smarter. I don't give up when I get knocked down, and I *always* keep moving forward—no matter what. Nothing can stop me.

Read that again and let it sink in. I have that painted in huge, bold letters on my office wall. I live it. I breathe it. I make sure that it is constantly in my mind and at the forefront for my entire team. And it works. Our company has grown from a scummy little shared office space and two people, to a spiffed-up, 3-story, 6500-square-foot building supporting 50 people and bringing in millions of dollars in revenue each year. I'm proud to say that we made INC's list of 5,000 fastest growing companies two years in a row. Not bad for a high school dropout.

"That's great, Engelo, but when are you actually going to give us some actionable advice?"

Ok, enough wind-blowing. Sorry!

Right now, mates. Read on.

It's a Numbers Game

Let's break things down a bit, starting with this point: It's all a numbers game.

Something that I tell everyone is that your success depends on how many hours you are willing to put in on a daily basis.

When are you going to get out of bed? When your alarm goes off, you get yourself out of bed. You go to the office, and you sit your butt in that office chair and you start at 6 a.m. You do not leave that office until 8 p.m. You put in 14-hour days—every single day, seven days a week, for two years minimum.

I don't care how dumb you think you are. I don't care how uneducated you are. It doesn't matter because in committing to those hours on a daily basis, you will eventually figure things out.

You'll learn who to call, what questions to ask, how to find people to invest in your deal, what to do once you get those partners. In the case of real estate, you'll learn things like what makes a good investment property, how to evaluate the costs and run the numbers, how to budget your renovation and stay on schedule—and most of all, how to make a tidy profit at the end of the day.

You'll figure out how to do one thing, which will lead to another, which will lead to a third, fourth, fifth—and before you know it, you will eventually understand how that process works, which will enable you to move on to the next piece of the puzzle. (Sorry to burst your bubble, guys, but there is no magic formula. I leave voodoo to the witch doctors and promises of overnight success to the scumbag "gurus.")

That is how I started in my real estate investing business. So, if it worked for me, why wouldn't it work for you? I started by sitting my butt in that office every single morning at 6 a.m. and I wouldn't leave until 8 p.m.

I have always been willing to put in that extra yard—and more than being willing to work longer and harder than everyone else, I actually follow through and do it. Always have, and always will.

OK, so let's say you are following that advice and putting in those 14-hour days. But here's an important point: What are you doing within those long hours? Now, if you are playing around with window blinds, like 99% of corporate America does (in my opinion)—along with filling their time with "poo-poo" breaks, long lunches and staring at the ceiling—well, that's not going to cut it. Obviously, you need to stay productive, right? You need to be focused within those hours.

Here's another of my quotes that I have ingrained in my psyche, and I suggest you also ingrain it in yours: "It takes a commitment of 80-plus hours per week—and an undivided focus within those hours—is ultimately what it comes down to."

Elon Musk, one of the greatest entrepreneurs alive right now, said that if the average person works 40 hours a week and wants to be a multimillionaire, that person needs to work 80 hours per week.

Why should anybody listen to that? Because Elon Musk is a freaking multi-multi-multi-multi-billionaire. Just in case you don't know (get out from under that rock, please), he co-founded PayPal and Tesla Inc. and is the founder and CEO of SpaceX, along with a lot of other ventures. A lot. At the time of this writing, Forbes puts his net worth at $19.7 billion. So I guess you can say that Elon Musk knows a bit about what he's talking about.

Now, I have added my twist to his statement to emphasize that you absolutely have to be focused. I have witnessed people in my office who have "worked" all day, but they haven't done diddly-squat, because they weren't focused. There has to be focus and action specific to your task or strategy within your commitment to those long hours. (By the way, I didn't let those people stick around long in my company.)

"Your Network Equals Your Net Worth"

Let's talk about some more numbers.

How many people do you speak to on a daily basis? (And I don't mean your family or friends.)

Real estate is a people business. Business in general is about people. You have to connect with people on a daily basis. There are numerous online real estate forums with many successful investors offering a wealth of knowledge. The more people you know and genuinely interact with, the more your mind will expand with knowledge, understanding and new ideas about how to approach your own goals and challenges.

Because you are going to hear opinions. You are going to hear suggestions. You are going to hear criticism. Take them all in and evaluate them, because they will make you better. They will make you a better real estate investor, a better entrepreneur and a better business owner.

Remember the old saying, "You are who you're with"? Who are you brushing shoulders with? Is it with your high school buddy "Bob" who smokes weed all day or your other buddy "Engelo" who flips more than 100 houses a year? Choose your associates wisely.

- How many hands do you shake on a daily basis?
- How many emails do you send?
- How many phone calls do you make?
- How many meetings do you attend?

I'm telling you, real estate is a numbers game. Take the emotion out of it and commit to the numbers. Work long. Work hard. Start early. Finish late. Send emails. Make phone calls. Attend meetings. Do videos. Write blogs. Become obsessed with everything and anything that is real estate-related. Nothing succeeds like excess when it comes to soaking up information about real estate.

How many times are you posting on social media? How many times does your newsletter get opened? How many people click? It's all a numbers game, guys.

How many offers do you submit on a daily basis? How are you going to buy a property unless you are out there submitting offers?

Ask yourself all of these questions over and over again. Commit to the numbers, mates. I'm telling you: They work.

Get Out of Your Comfort Zone

I don't have to tell you it's hard to change your way of doing things. Maybe you've become complacent, settling for results that are "good enough." Why push yourself? Because you can do better! Because when you reach those higher goals, you get rewards. Maybe it's money; maybe it's the overwhelming confidence that comes with having finished that half-marathon and knowing that yes, you can do the full 26.2 miles next time. Either way, it feels great, doesn't it? And that motivates you to keep on reaching for even loftier goals with even bigger and better rewards.

So why doesn't everybody get out of their comfort zone? Why don't people break out of the status quo? Because it takes effort, commitment and perseverance. And too many people—I hate to have to say it again—are lazy, risk-averse a-holes!

Here's a good example: Think about how many people commit to losing weight as a New Year's resolution. People are packed like sardines into gyms and health clubs every January and into February. But look inside those gyms when March rolls around—those places are practically deserted! Where did everybody go? Why did all those people give up? Here's why: Because it just got too hard. Other stupid stuff like watching TV gets in the way.

Seriously? How lame can you get?! Come on...

If you want to lose weight, you go to the gym—daily. You get on the treadmill. And you change your eating habits, starting with cutting out carbs and sugar. Those things take commitment, and it's not easy. I know. It must become a new lifestyle and not just something you do for a short amount of time (But consult your own health practitioner about these things, because I'm not a medical doctor. I'm only the "Dr. of Real Estate Investing")

Take it to the Limit—One More Time

Here's a quick tip for you: If you're someone who's hitting the gym—running, lifting weights, spinning, doing the treadmill, whatever—and when you finish your workout you say to yourself, "That wasn't so bad," then you're not doing it right and you're "fluffing out."

I said get out of your freaking comfort zone! Push yourself to the limit and don't stop even then. Push yourself past your limit! It's the un-aerobic level of heart rate of 180+ that you want to reach.

When you're on that treadmill, or if you are running for 10 miles, it's not the first nine miles that's building your fitness. It's the 10th mile, mates! When you're bench-pressing to build muscle, it's not the first nine repetitions that you are pushing out easily that are making a difference. It's that last repetition—the one that you can hardly push out. The one where you need someone to spot you. That's where you build the most muscle.

And in the office, it's not the first 99 phone calls that get you a sale or a deal. It's the last phone call—when you are tired and you cannot do any more, but you pick up that phone one last time, and you reluctantly dial the number and you get the deal. It's happened to me many times. True story. I call it the "magic of the 11th hour."

Bill Rancic, a well-known entrepreneur, motivational speaker and author, said at an event in Chicago that the number one thing that worked for him in business was this: When you're done and can't do it anymore—maybe you're sick of the whole day and you've been getting absolutely blasted by everything and everyone—that's when you need to just do that "one more thing." Just that one last thing that will set you apart from everyone else. Whatever it is. Maybe it's that one last email. Or one more phone call. Or social media post. Or meeting. Maybe it's staying that extra hour.

It's that one last thing that you do when you cannot do any more. It's called getting out of your comfort zone. You have to push yourself through that limit. And when you can push yourself and you can go beyond your comfort zone, that is when true miracles will happen for you, in every shape and form. They truly will—in real estate, in business, in your personal life.

You probably are familiar with the image of that guy searching for gold who gets ever-so-close but then puts that pickax on his back and just walks away. And then there is that other guy who's madly pushing through. His perseverance is going to pay off and he's going to hit pay dirt because he keeps chipping away even when he thinks he can't do it anymore. I want you to be that person. Every single day you have to tell yourself, "If I give up now, I could be that guy who was that close to success, that close to striking gold but walked away when that one last swing could have made me rich."

You are never allowed to give up. You have to keep pushing on and pushing through, even when you think you can't do it anymore. Never stop. Always be out of your comfort zone, because when you truly get out of your comfort zone, that's when the magic happens. It honestly does.

And that is *The Raw Truth*.

Actions Produce Results

Next point: Actions speak louder than words. Don't just talk the talk; you've got to walk the walk. Follow through and do what you say you're going to do.

Successful people respect people who do what they say they're going to do. And that's how I conduct myself, too, in whatever it is that I want to accomplish.

Even if you fail miserably. It doesn't matter, because at least you gave it a shot. No regrets, guys.

I love this quote: "Ever tried? Ever failed? No matter. Try again. Fail again. Fail better."

For crying out loud, I cannot even count the number of people I have heard talking the talk, but that's where it stops. They're big blabbermouths who never back up what they say with any concrete action. They never *do* anything—in business or in life. Do you know any such people?

Ultimately, your actions speak louder than your words. You don't need to be loud (unless it complements your brain like it does mine!). Just shut your big, fat mouth, put your head down and get the job done. Don't say it. Just do it! Better than Nike!

Here's one of my favorite sayings: "Stop being a 'Johnny Talker.' Become a Johnny Walker and make it Blue with two ice cubes." (Yeah, I'm full of quotes, but I know you love them.)

Why are there so many people out there who talk the talk, but are not willing to walk the walk or to take action? It goes back to the idea of the comfort zone. They're scared to try something they haven't done before or that's unfamiliar to them or their routine. They like flirting with the idea, but they are just too terrified of failing.

Working a 9-to-5 job is comfortable, isn't it, mates? Going out and starting your own business is uncomfortable because you don't always know where that next paycheck is coming from or when it's coming in. But ultimately, pressure builds diamonds—if you can handle the pressure.

Maybe you're existing comfortably in that preordained life journey that society has laid out for you. You know the one: Go to college, get a 9-to-5 job, get married, buy a house, have a baby, upsize house, downsize to afford kids' college, drop dead after spending the peanuts in your 401(k). When something out of the ordinary or risky presents itself, you say, "Oh, no, I can't do that. I might fail. I can't have people judging me like that."

My mates, life is impermanent. We all end up in the same place. Don't live a life of regrets. It's better to live a life of failure than of regrets. You will succeed, though. I believe in you.

It's far better to do something new and maybe fall short than it is to not even try. If you don't take action, you'll never know.

Besides, failing is not always a bad thing. I've made some colossal missteps—some unbelievably huge failures—in my life and in business. But those are the ones I've learned the most from. Failing—and really studying and understanding why you failed—enables you to adjust your plans, to try again and ultimately to succeed.

Now let me ask you: When you try something and it doesn't work out, do you look at that as a bad experience? Do you immediately run away? I'll bet most of you do. But you don't have to. And you shouldn't, in my opinion. I don't.

I have trained my mind to think this way: "Every experience is a good experience as long as you perceive it to be a good experience."

You should let that statement guide you in every action.

Let me give you an example. Let's say you start a business. You hustle for three years and you end up losing $250,000. The first thing that comes to your mind is that it has been a bad experience. No, it hasn't!

Think about it: An experience in and of itself is neither good nor bad—it's simply an experience. It's your mind that colors your perception and makes you think it was good or bad. What you need to do in the case of our example is find whatever was good within that sordid horror story of losing $250,000. That is what you are going to feed yourself with. That is what you are going take and use to push forward to try again.

Take that lesson and use it as leverage to propel yourself into the next thing, into the next business or deal. Don't let it drown you. Don't dwell on it for too long. Think about it—yes; you have to. You have to dissect it. You have to understand what went wrong, but then you have to comfort your soul by finding something good from within it. Don't let the negative energy of failure drag you down.

That's what helps me push to the next thing. When I take action and I fail, I have to dissect that failure. But then I tell myself, "You know what? I am never going to make that same mistake again. I may have lost $25,000 on that business venture, but guess what? I am not going to lose that $250,000 on my next deal, when it really, really counts." And why I am not going to lose that $250,000? Because I made that mistake on $25,000. And to me, that makes it a definitely positive experience!

Here's another quote I love: "Run to your fears." Are you afraid of failing? Then run straight toward that fear. Confront your failure. Embrace it. Put it under a microscope and learn everything you can about it.

Here's another way to look at it: You could start 100 times and fail 99. Succeed only once and that "once" could lead to the next Amazon, Microsoft, Facebook, etc. It doesn't matter how many times you're wrong, as long as you're right once and it counts. Never give up!

Here's why failing is so important: Because you are *not* going make that same sort of careful examination of your successes. When you make money, be it in real estate or in business, you don't evaluate what caused you to make that financial gain or profitable real estate transaction, because your ego is blossoming. You are on top of the world, and you are not going to break down every little step of the way that caused that financial gain or profit on that particular transaction. Because you are too busy thinking about that Rolex, or that Porsche, or buying your spouse some nice designer clothes or going on holiday. So success and being successful don't really teach you anything. They just make your ego blossom and can turn you into a cocky, arrogant jerk over the long term.

They say that more money just magnifies who you already are. I believe that to be true. But when you fail, now that is brilliant. That is beautiful.

I absolutely love failing! And do you know why? Because when I do, I feel like hell. I am upset and embarrassed and it starts to make me think. I can't sleep. I can't eat. I am haunted by my failure. And so I break down every little step that caused that failure. Every email, phone call, every single minute, I break those things down in my head and I replay the entire scenario over and over and over and over and over again.

Now, I ask you, after you have dissected a failure like that to the finest detail, what are you going to do? Are you going to repeat the same mistakes? No; I can guarantee you that you aren't. Not unless you're insane, since, as the saying goes, "Insanity is doing the same thing over and over again and expecting a different result." (If you are insane, I suggest reading a different book.)

No Regrets!

So don't be afraid to take action just because there's a chance you might fail. Dare to take risks, or you may spend your golden years wondering, "What if?" like the retirees in one study who were asked about their biggest regret in life.

They were asked, "If you could roll back the film on your life and go back to when you were 20 to 30 years old, what would you do differently? Would you spend more time with family? Would you go on more holidays? Would you try to get a better job? Would you get a higher college degree?"

Many of these elderly folks said they would have taken more risk throughout their younger years. What exactly does that mean? That could mean not being chained to a house with a mortgage for 30 years. That could mean telling your heartless, demanding boss to get lost, and starting your own business. That could mean going to the Bahamas and living there for two years, if that's what you really want to do.

All these things are risks. And if you don't take action, they will be your regrets when you are sitting in that rocking chair when you're 80 or 90 years old. (If you're lucky enough to live that long…)

I can tell you right now, I personally don't want to live my life thinking, "What if?" I know I sound crazy with some of the things I want to do, but I still back up whatever I say with action and then I deal with the consequences of whatever my actions bring. So far, I have failed so many times that I've lost count, but guess what? That means I tried. I didn't just talk the talk; I walked the walk. I took action.

And I wasn't scared to fail.

Now get me that Johnny Walker Blue with two ice cubes.

P.S. You can always go back to your lousy 9-to-5 if you suck at business or real estate.

"It's impossible,' said pride. 'It's risky,' said experience.
'It's pointless,' said reason. 'Give it a try,' said the heart."
— Unknown

Chapter 2

THE "AMERICAN DREAM" IS DEAD

We just spent the last however-many pages talking about taking action. About hustling. About sacrificing. About working really ... *really* ... excruciatingly ... hard!

But how many people out there have taken the time to stop and think about what they're working for?

And even if you do know the "what," can you answer the "why?"

Are you working your butt off because it's leading to what you really want? Or are you doing it out of some sense of responsibility to live up to what your parents always wanted—and pushed—you to be or to do? Or to fulfill society's perception of what you should be doing?

Wait—I've got it. I've read the script a hundred times. I know how you've got your life planned out, and I'll bet it goes something like this:

- Make good grades in school. (Mom: "Did you do your home-work, Johnny?")
- Get into a good college. (Dad: "Son, follow in my footsteps and go to Harvard.")
- Graduate with your degree. (You: "Great. I majored in sociol-ogy. I wonder what jobs there are out there.")
- Land a great job. (You: "I guess working as a sales rep at Ver-izon will do for now.")
- Find a partner and get married. (You: "I have to get married before I'm 30 because my parents did.")
- Buy a house. (You: "How the hell do we afford that mort-gage?")
- Have a family. (You: "Oops; that was two accidents.")
- Move to the suburbs so the kids can go to a great school. (You: "But I really want to travel and live in the Bahamas.")
- Get a better job that pays more money so you can afford that house in the suburbs. (You: "Woohoo! I'm the store manager at Verizon.")
- Buy a bigger house for your growing family. Or to keep up with the Joneses. (Wife: "Honey, I really like this house." You: "How the blazes do we afford that mortgage?")
- Get a job that pays even more money—even if you don't like the job—so you can pay for that bigger mortgage. (You: "I never really liked Verizon anyway. Regional Manager at AT&T is so much better. I get company stock and I only work 100 hours a week for no extra pay!")
- Then, downsize because you need extra money to afford your children's college tuition. (You: My dad went to college and I went to college, so I guess my kids need to go, also.")
- Retire and (you hope!) have enough money to last you for the rest of your life. (You: "OK, I'm 60 years old and I have

$150,000 in my retirement account. How long do you think I'll live for?" Engelo: "You never even lived, mate...")
- And then? You just drop dead. (Engelo: "What a lame life, if you ask me...")

The American Dream, right?

Well, if that's your version of the American Dream, let me clue you in on something—and I warn you, this may be hard for you to hear: The American Dream is dead. It's false. It's fake. Don't get sucked into that line of B.S.!

Society Has Brainwashed You

Crikey, mate! Get your head out of the sand and think about it!

The American Dream is something "society" came up with and has been brainwashing generation after generation to believe.

Your parents brainwashed you from an early age into believing it.

That's because their parents brainwashed them. Because their parents brainwashed them before that. Because ... well, you get the idea.

If you want to be truly happy and successful in life, slam on the brakes! Right now!

Get off that hamster wheel and think about what you want. Look deep within and determine what you really want. And that will help by setting the best path for you to follow to achieve it. Living abroad for two years? Driving a fancy car while you're still young? Whatever it is, listen and follow your heart.

I am so fortunate and so grateful that my own mother never fell for that Stepford rubbish—falling in line with the all the other mothers who mindlessly repeated the same rules for their children just because it was the societal norm.

As I was growing up, she told me, "Engelo, the grades that you get in school will really never have anything to do with your success in life." And I will always remember this saying: "Formal education will earn you a living, while personal development will give you a lifestyle." (There I go again with another quote!)

Because my mother wisely knew that, she didn't force me to go to school under pressure in the same way that a lot of other parents forced their kids to go to school—all in pursuit of the almighty straight-A report card and all kinds of other meaningless academic honors.

I am so grateful that she didn't force me to sit at home and do my homework, but instead let me just go out and play soccer. Because I loved soccer. That's what I really wanted to do. She let me be free. She let me do what I wanted to do, in the way I wanted to do it. That enabled me to achieve my dream of being a professional soccer player. And that ability to succeed at what I wanted to do laid the groundwork for what I am doing today. (Side note/tip for all the mommies and daddies reading this: Check out Montessori schools for your kids. It's a game changer in the educational system.)

A lot of other kids buckle under the pressure to get good grades, to go to school, to get a degree, to accomplish all of these things just so their parents can pat themselves on the back. And when someone is constantly pushing you to do something that you don't want to do, eventually you become like a donkey that suddenly parks itself in the middle of the road and refuses to move. You become like that donkey because you have been hit so hard, too many times. You don't want to move anymore. You're done. And I pray that you don't go down the wrong path in life, just like so many of my childhood friends have done.

So, maybe you've done alright, gotten a college degree, a decent job, that 5-bedroom, 2 1/2-bath suburban "dream home." Maybe you're earning a living that society deems acceptable. But what about you? Are you happy? Are you fulfilled? Is this what you really want? (Look deep within; what do you really want?)

Maybe you think success is moving into that big house in the suburbs—with that accompanying big mortgage, by the way. You think you will finally have made it; you will have achieved the American Dream.

Well, think again.

The Real Story

Here's what happens once you're in that big house with that big mortgage: You're stuck there—in that same nondescript, boring property—for 20–30 years, most likely.

Then your kids grow up, and you need extra money to afford their college educations. So you downsize. (Most likely to an apartment or townhouse in the same suburb. Have you ever even traveled overseas to Europe, Johnny boy?) A few years later, the kids are out.

You're probably 60 years old by then. You've downsized. You and your spouse (I hope you're still married, by the way—the divorce rate is unbelievably high!) have worked maybe 40 hours a week for 40 long years. If you're lucky, you have enough money—20% of your income—saved for retirement. More likely, though, you're one of the majority who find themselves without a big enough nest egg.

Because for those 40 or so years, you've been doing your best just to stay ahead—to put food on the table, a roof over your family's heads, pay the rent/mortgage, keep the car running, get out of credit card debt, pay off student loans and/or help your parents/children/siblings. If you're lucky, you may have achieved a higher spot on the corporate ladder that has provided you a bit of discretionary income, but then that gets eaten up by vacations, weekend entertainment and everything else that goes along with showing others your status in life. You probably are not even enjoying your personal life. Why? Because you're tethered to that 9-to-5 job from 7-to-7 (or longer, making your boss richer and richer with every working hour)—even most weekends—so that you can make enough money to pay for all those things your spouse and kids think they have to have to fit in with their peers.

The American Dream? More like an American Nightmare, if you ask me!

Aren't these supposed to be your "golden years"—now that you've gotten the kids out and on their own? And yet here you are, still struggling, with hardly enough money to scrape by. And guess what happens next? You simply drop dead! That's right. Done, gone, dusted, bye-bye, finito.

There's your American dream, everybody! That's what you're chasing! For heaven's sake: WAKE UP!

You Can Change the Script

The good news is that there is a better way. Your way.

I'm not saying don't go to college—if that's what you want. But study what you want to study, what you are interested in. Go for a career that you want—or don't even bother with a career. Start a business, start a charity, hit "pause" and backpack around the world.

Live your own dream—not somebody else's.

Do whatever makes you happy.

You want to be rich? Guess what? So do I! So do a lot of people. But that doesn't mean you have to chase that ridiculous American Dream of owning that 3,000-square-foot, 5-bedroom, 2½-bath suburban home. (That's not a measurement of being "rich.")

Allow me to let you in on a little secret: You actually can get rich quicker by not getting suckered into buying a house.

Without a house and mortgage dragging you down like a sinking anchor, you can be in control of your destiny. And your happiness. That's right—you!

Being happy is being rich.

You can have the career you want, whether it's real estate or something else. You've got mobility. Don't like where you're living? Got annoying jerks for neighbors? Tell 'em to go jump in the lake and then just pick up and move. Feel like exploring the Bahamas for three months? Off you go. Now, that's freedom! (If you can't tell, I'm a big fan of the Bahamas.)

Look at me, for example, mates. I don't care one bit about owning my own personal place of residence. And it doesn't matter to me what anyone else says, because I don't care about living the American Dream. Here's what I do want: I want to live *my* dream, and I encourage you to do the same.

I'm not beholden to society's norms, or to sticking with the status quo. Success comes from doing things differently and being different, in my opinion.

That's why—even though I am successfully running two multi-million-dollar companies—I am quite satisfied to be spending 14-hour days hustling my tail off (I'm thinking about slowing down a bit soon. "Retirement" sounds good to me at 35 years old. Thoughts?), and coming home to a little 2-bedroom, 1-bathroom rental apartment for myself, my wife and my daughter.

It's all part of a bigger, very well thought out plan, with this foundational principle: No leverage!

"No, he didn't just say that..."

Impossible, you say? Not at all, mates. You, too, can make money in real estate investing without using any leverage.

"What?"

Allow me to explain the magic behind my plan, using what I call my "green little soldiers" as an example. (Get your calculator out because you probably don't remember any of this math stuff from your school days.)

Let's say your dream is to own a half-million-dollar property in the suburbs. (If that truly is your dream.) If you were to buy that $500,000 property with leverage, you'd need to put down $100,000 (hypothetically), which is 20 percent.

Now let's think of each one of those hundred thousand dollars as a green little soldier.

As soon as you put $100,000 as a down payment on that half-million-dollar property, you are putting your 100,000 green little soldiers into a bunker. ("Intangible equity"—Google it if you don't know what it means, lazy!) And your green little soldiers are getting rusty. Their rifles are getting rusty, and they're not doing anything worthwhile. They are sitting in that bunker playing cards.

You can talk to me all day long about how you are paying off that mortgage and you don't have to pay rent because the mortgage payments are actually going toward paying off that property and it's better to pay a mortgage than rent because rent is gone forever, blah, blah, blah.

Pardon my frankness, but that's total B.S. Your mortgage payments are actually going toward interest payments, and if you look at how much in interest you pay over a 30-year mortgage, it is frighteningly ridiculous. Not just that, you're also covering all expenses on that property. You're having to pay for all of the taxes on that property, insurance, repairs, etc. So, you're not only dealing with the mortgage payment, you also have to eat a lot of other fees and costs associated with maintaining that property.

Now look at someone like me, for example. I rent. I pay $700 per month (yep, it's gone forever, but I don't care), but with my $100,000—my 100,000 green little soldiers—I go out and buy, fix and flip one property. That adds another $20,000 profit to my tally. I buy, fix and flip another property. That adds another $20,000.

Let's just say I buy, fix and flip five houses in one year. At the end of that year, I have 200,000 green little soldiers. But you, who put $100,000 down on your 5-bedroom mansion, still only have an army of 100,000 green little soldiers that are quietly rusting away. You'd better hope the market doesn't take a nosedive, because that could mean 100,000 *dead* soldiers. The point here is to make capital gains with the existing money that you already have, and I hope this book helps you do just that. (Note: Don't be a smart aleck and say that I didn't estimate paying taxes on the profits in my example above. I'm not an accountant and am just using this as a "fool-proof" example.)

Remember This: Money Makes Money

Aside from not gaining any value, that decision to use leverage is costing you more in interest, maintenance and all kinds of other miscellaneous junk fees. (Even LMI—"Lenders Mortgage Insurance"— fees, if your down payment is less than 20%.)

The only cost that I have is rent. Not just that, if I don't like that rental, you know what I can do? After one year, or however long my lease runs, I can move wherever I want to. If I work in a profession and I get a job offer with 50% more pay, I can also move easily. Even as a business owner, maybe I stumble across a new exciting venture or a new/better and more profitable opportunity in another market.

I've got mobility. I've got freedom. Think about it; nations fight wars for freedom. But you've got none, my mate. You're stuck in that house for the next 30 years and you've got an ax over your head forcing you to get out of bed every day to trudge off to that mindless job that you can't leave because you have to repay that monster mortgage.

In order to achieve any kind of success in life, you have to make sacrifices. It's just *The Raw Truth*.

For me, that sacrifice is renting a smaller property that I might not really want to be renting, but it allows me to invest my hard-earned cash so it will multiply and grow my army of green little soldiers.

My green little soldiers are fighting for me at any and every given moment. They are conquering new territory. And multiplying. They're not getting rusty. They are constantly fighting—every day, every week, every month. Sometimes some of them die (yes, you can lose money in real estate). But more join the ranks soon. While I sleep, they still keep fighting. I am getting richer. And richer.

And consider this: I started off with practically nothing. I scraped together $50,000 as the initial money I used to start my real estate endeavors.

I'll say it again: Money makes money. Never forget that!

When you really break down the numbers, you can see that it is much more profitable in the long run to rent and invest than it is to buy and own. No ifs, ands or buts about it.

And it doesn't have to be just flipping investment properties. You can grow your army of green little soldiers with a buy-hold-rent strategy, too.

Instead of putting $100,000 into a mortgage, you're better off buying, fixing and tenanting one property for $50,000 and another property for $50,000, because of the cash flow coming in. (It's possible. Check out the Midwest. There are deals there like that falling off trees.)

Let's just say that there's a 10 percent net return on your investment of $100,000. That's $10,000 a year that you are getting back in cash flow. What if instead of doing that, you put that $100,000 into a mortgage? What happens if you lose your job? (Just ask all of the folks that have ever experienced a foreclosure.) Who's going to pay your mortgage? You're screwed. But if you lose your job while you are renting but you also own those two investment properties, you've still got your rent covered. How? By the money coming in from those two investment properties. (Please be reasonable like I am with my $700 per month rental now and don't live in Beverly Hills because the cash flow won't even cover the monthly landscaping bill.) As I mentioned before, it really comes down to investing your money well and for high capital gain returns or high cash flow.

It's a very simple calculation. And it also shows why it's safer to rent and invest than to buy and own.

So let's sum things up, here:

We're all chasing something. What are you chasing? Why are you chasing that? Is that your dream, or somebody else's?

Look deep, deep down inside yourself. Remember back to when you were a kid, when you had big dreams for your life and nobody had yet passed any judgment on whether those dreams were good or bad, attainable or not attainable, acceptable or not acceptable.

When you look deeply into your soul like that, that's when you can recapture your dreams. And then, here's what you do: Move heaven and earth to reach them. Don't let anything or anybody stand in your way. Focus on the "what" and never forget the "why."

It won't always be easy. Success takes sacrifice. You'll have to work your butt off. But you can do it. And it's worth it.

Just make sure it's what you *really* want.

"I'm a great believer in luck, and I find the harder I work,
the more I have of it."
— Thomas Jefferson

Chapter 3

CASH IS KING

I know you've seen those social media ad "snippet" videos with punks riding in super cars, which all are a variation of this:

"No money? Hey, no problem! Let me show you how you, too, can earn a million dollars in real estate without investing a dime of your own!" Hell, as long as we're at it, why not make it $5 million? Or $10 million? Throw in a Lambo, also. And some of those con artists *do* claim that!

You know what I say to that? Give me a break! Who do those shysters think they're kidding? And who do you think you're kidding if you're gullible enough to fall for any of that B.S.? The only thing that any of those folks are good at is social media marketing. Period.

Sure, I know it sounds great—and don't we all wish it could be true?—but face it: You don't get something for nothing. Not here. Not there. Not anywhere. And especially not in real estate investing. That's the simple, *Raw Truth*. Here's what you get when you have nothing to put into the deal: Nada. Zilch. Zippo. Zero. Or to put it another way: You're still as broke as when you started. (Unless, of course, you're a thief, which will make you end up in the banger with Bubba.)

Then, why do so many people get suckered into these get-rich-quick traps? I'll tell you why. Because everybody wants something for nothing. They're lazy sons-of-guns. In fact, far too many people I encounter think the world owes them a free ride. Really?!? It makes me absolutely sick. My American mates, this country is the best in the world, and you are blessed to be here (just ask all of the folks in third-world countries). It owes you nothing, but rather you "owe" it for the privilege of living here.

So many people I speak to are all looking for a magic pill: "I am going to pop the blue pill and I'll be able to go out and make money without having any money." Like low-money or no-money-down investment strategies. You've got to be kidding! How can anybody possibly think you can actually make money without having any money? That is mind-boggling to me. I guess they are all just good clickbait titles to increase views and sell books.

They're looking for the easy way out: "I want to do the least amount of work and get the most amount of reward." Well, guess what? Here is a wake-up call for all those misguided twits out there (and I don't want you to be one of them): That's not how it works. It never has, and it never will. Wake up to a thing called "life," where nothing is free.

If you've been paying attention in the chapters leading up to this one, you know success in real estate—as in any worthwhile endeavor—takes hard work. And commitment. And sacrifice.

That's what being an entrepreneur is all about. I'm sorry that seems to be such a foreign concept to the masses out there; they just don't understand. Some of them think it's about posing for photos in front of a rented car. What a joke. So brace yourself, if you truly want to be a successful entrepreneur: You are going to be misunderstood. And for extended periods of time.

While you're working 6 a.m. to 10 p.m., attending real estate investor meet-ups, shadowing people who've been out there and are willing to show you the ropes, researching through books and online forums—*and by doing*! —while you have your time and attention consumed by all that, you're going to be surrounded by people who don't get it. They can't fathom what you're trying to accomplish. They don't understand why you can't drop everything to join them for happy hour on 10 minutes' notice, or to go dancing, or to the soccer game, or the movies, or whatever it may be. They've got time; so, why don't you?

Remember, they think they're getting everything for nothing, so of course they've got all the time in the world. They're content to play it safe at a boring 9-to-5 job (which they hate, by the way), brainwashed by society to think there's one, true path to achieving the American Dream (work, buy a house, get into major debt, get saddled with a mortgage and imprisoned by an unchallenging job—just because everyone else is spending money on liabilities like a car, clothes, boat, etc.). As long as they have no vision, passion or a desire for something more, they will never understand what you're doing or where you're going. But it doesn't matter.

It may be a lonely road to the top, but believe me, reaching your destination is worth every bit of blood, sweat and tears you experience on the way. So, savor every moment of that journey. You will cherish the memories with a big grin on your face.

Now that we've set the stage and got you pumped up—I warned you I was going to lay it all out and tell it like it really is!—are you ready for some actionable advice from your mate who's traveled that lonely, rocky road and knows what kind of sacrifice it takes to achieve your dream?

Beware the Hucksters

OK, then. First—if I haven't made it clear enough to you already—don't fall for that get-rich-quick (or should I say, get-rich-without-lifting-a-finger) line from some slimy, snake-oil-peddling, car-renting guru who says you can be successful in real estate without having any kind of capital. Forget about it. It's a lie. That dream world doesn't exist, and the odds of doing it legitimately and successfully are very, very small.

And it's not just the gurus selling their "secret formula" for making money without having any money. It's also the hard-money lenders out there who make it seem so easy to come up with financing for your deal—but who will then charge you an arm and a leg *and* won't hesitate to call your note if you're late. Remember my guiding rule: *No leverage!* Only cold, hard cash that you have painstakingly and methodically saved. (Nothing beats hard work.)

Here is what you need to do: You need to go out and hustle your butt off in your 9-to-5 job. And get yourself another job, too, while you're at it. I'm not kidding. You need to work day and night. (I'll bet no one ever told you that, did they?) You need to be frugal. Put away every single penny you possibly can. Don't spend money on stupid stuff. There is too much debt in this country already, so don't be another statistic.

I find it absolutely crazy that the average U.S. household's consumer debt (including credit cards, mortgage, car loans, etc.) is $135,065. That's according to NerdWallet's 2018 annual analysis of U.S. household debt. What the hell?!? Don't be dumb! Have no debt.

And as if that weren't bad enough, GOBankingRates.com's 2018 Retirement Savings Survey found that 42 percent of Americans have less than $10,000 saved. And of that group, 14% reported that they have *nothing at all* saved. Unbelievable!! Granted, many of the under-$10,000 group are millennials, so they've got plenty of catch-up time. But it's not so easy for those nearing—or in the midst of—retirement.

Work hard, be debt-free, stay frugal and save! Once you have saved $50,000 to $100,000 in cash—cold, hard cash—then you can actually use that money and go out and do something. But not before then. Until you have saved that much money, we've got nothing to talk about. Don't even read this book. (Well, you're kind of hooked now, so you might as well finish it.) Seriously, though, there is nothing I can do to help you until you have some capital to work with. I'm sorry...

But take it from a guy who's been penniless, a guy who's had nothing to his name except a very focused entrepreneurial vision: You can do it! I promise that you can. Keep reading, and I'll keep helping.

First of all, simply confronting the challenge of hard work in the first place will teach you a great deal about what it takes to succeed. There's no substitute for the firsthand sacrifice of not going out for drinks with friends or going for that dinner. It's not easy, but you'll begin to see the rewards of working hard, saving money and being frugal. And that will spur you to keep at it. Your savings will slowly but surely start to grow and get closer to that $50,000 to $100,000 in free-and-clear cash that you'll need to start investing.

Prove to yourself first that you can work hard and save smart before trying your hand at any real estate investment strategy. In my eyes, it's the foundation that every investor needs to have before they start building the framework.

Now, when you finally do have that cash, that doesn't mean go out and plunk it down on the first deal that comes along. You have to be patient. When I was starting out, I wasn't patient, and I lost my shirt—and then some! But that was a great learning experience for me and now I can use that knowledge to help you.

Steering Clear of Pitfalls

Rushing into a bad deal disguised as a great one—without taking time to research and do the proper due diligence—was one of the biggest mistakes that I made in my real estate investing career. I needed to buy that next deal, or so I convinced myself. Just to add quantity to my portfolio, just to be able to tell people I was this super-awesome real estate investor who owned a ton of real estate, just so that I could prove people wrong when they said I'd never amount to anything. That mental complex sure did cost me a lot of time and money.

But I was the one who was wrong. I was wrong to not wait for the right deal to come along in the right area that I could buy for the right price, that needed the right amount of rehab work, that I could then sell for a very large profit. Or where I could refinance out of that property and use that money to go into another transaction.

The key is that you need to determine your end goal *before you start*.

How do you do that, you're probably asking. It involves some future-casting. You've got your vision, right? You know what you ultimately want to achieve, whether it's five years, or 10, or 20 down the road. That's the first step: Determine your cash-flow end goal and where you want to be. Then you can reverse-engineer and break down the steps of how to reach that goal.

Here's a hypothetical example:

Ten years from now, you want to be earning $10,000 per month—or $120,000 a year—in passive income. Let's say that's a 10 percent return on your invested dollars. (I'm keeping things super-simple. Sorry to all the "heroes" out there who are after complex Einstein-level math equations and calculations B.S.) So, in order to make $10,000 per month, you are going to need to have $1.2 million in cold, hard cash invested and working for you at a 10 percent net return per annum. Make sense? If not, well, to hell with it! Get your calculator out, already…

But that is what's happening 10 years from now! What about today?

Well, today, you have $50,000 to $100,000 that you have saved by working your butt off while all your friends were partying into the wee hours every night. (All they have is a killer hangover once they finally do wake up. If they don't "wake up" soon, that "hangover" will last them forever. But back to our example...)

The question is, how can you use the money you have now so that in 10 years you will have $1.2 million? Can you get there by buying a house, putting a down payment on it? No, that won't help you reach your end goal. What about buying and holding? Nope, that probably won't work, either. You need other strategies. You need to buy, fix and flip. And you might need to wholesale. You might need to do those things and still work part-time (as a real estate agent, maybe?) to make additional income. You might need to invest in the stock market when it tanks. (Ride the wave up.) You might need to start a business that can produce cash flow and profits. Even a side hustle. Do whatever it takes; just don't rob a bank or commit any crimes.

There's no single, right way to do it; there are various possibilities. What you need to do is research all those possibilities to see what makes sense for you and what you feel most comfortable with. This book isn't about breaking down every investment strategy to its finer details. I'll let you go down the same rabbit hole that I've been down, called "investing."

If you're looking at a buy-and-hold strategy, for instance, you need to break things down so you can determine how many properties will be needed to produce the cash flow to give you that $10,000 per month.

But I don't think that $50,000 to $100,000 of cash right now is going to be enough for you to buy and hold immediately. So what do you do? Assuming you chose real estate investing, your approach needs to be that every property you buy is going to bring you a step closer to achieving your end goal.

For instance, let's say a property comes along that you can buy for $30,000, renovate for $20,000, and sell for $80,000. (I do deals like this all day long. Yes, move, if necessary, to start doing deals in another market where you can, too.) The world is your oyster when you don't anchor yourself to a house mortgage. After all costs, you make around $20,000 in net profit. Is that a good deal? It is when you consider that if you do that five times a year, and make $20,000 on each deal, that's $100,000 in profit per annum with the $50,000 in savings that you started out with.

Now if you do that for 10 years (and we're not including taxes here, or potential for capital appreciation, for that matter—I'm trying to keep these numbers very simple, so please forgive me if you're a super-analytical type), you will make $1 million in profit. Since your end goal was to make $1.2 million, you fell a little bit short. So, go back to the drawing board to see how you could increase your profit. Maybe you should look at doing six deals a year, rather than five, or the remainder can be made up by some properties that you don't sell and decide to hold for cash flow. That would give you $120,000 or so in profit per year so that after 10 years, you have hit your goal of $1.2 million. Now that's success *and* piña coladas!

It's All About the Bigger Picture

That is how to invest in real estate—with the bigger picture in mind. Every deal you contemplate has to get you a step closer to achieving your end goal. Don't invest just for the sake of being able to say you're investing. Instead, have a definite end goal. Fast-forward into the future to determine where you want to be. Then be patient! Wait for that right deal to come along. I speak to a ton of investors from all over the world on a daily basis and almost all of them fail to paint a clear picture of where they want to be and how much passive income they want to earn. Paint your future before investing and make sure it's a masterpiece.

One of the biggest mistakes I have made as a real estate investor—and I have made a lot of them!—was being too impatient. Let me tell you, I don't make that mistake anymore. And I don't want you to make it at all.

Also, don't feel bad for missing out on a "good deal," because there will always be another deal around the corner. I promise. Just don't rush.

Etch this into your mind and let it guide you in every deal you do: Money makes money. You've got to start with some before you can make more. And that means working hard, living frugally, and saving every single spare penny you can until you have that $50,000 to $100,000 in cold hard cash to start you on your investing journey.

Cash is king, my mates. And I want all of you to be royalty.

"9-to-5 is just survival. What you do before 9 a.m.
and after 5 p.m. is what matters most.
This is bigger-picture thinking and doing."
— Engelo Rumora

Chapter 4

CASH FLOW IS THE QUEEN

If cash is king, then cash flow is queen. And with both as your "parents," you get to be a prince/princess (royalty). Now, what do I mean by that? I mean simply that the two go hand in hand. You need one (cash) to generate the other (cash flow). And together, they pack one powerful punch!

In real estate—unlike the dilemma of the chicken or the egg—you *do* know which one comes first: Cash. Cold, hard cash. We've already established that, in the previous chapter. Without money, you can't make money, because you've got no starting point.

But once you have that $50,000 to $100,000 that you're going to save by working your tail off, then you can make your first investment. And remember, you're making a carefully thought-out, wise investment that will suit your end goal. You want that first investment to start the momentum that will grow your cash and in essence your cash flow as well.

Then you'll have even more money available to do more investment deals, which will increase your cash flow. See how it works? It's absolutely beautiful! A royal money-making machine!

But let me back up for just a minute to how you use cash flow to achieve your end goal. Because as much as we might like it to, this process does not happen automatically or by magic.

We have talked in a general way in the previous chapters about focusing on your end goal first, then determining the best course of action (or investing strategy) to make it happen. It's a matter of basic calculations once you know the amount of money you want to end up with and the amount of time in which you want to achieve that goal. When it comes to real estate investing as your strategy, you plug the appropriate numbers—purchase price, rent, expenses, etc.—into a formula. (There are many different formulas for calculating different things when investing in real estate.)

I've brought it down to simple and practical terms for the sake of explaining the concept, but in reality, it's a much-more-involved process. (Isn't everything?!)

Hoping is Not a Strategy

A single, unshakable piece of guidance to use in every situation is this: Do not ever—and I mean never, ever, ever, EVER—base your calculations on capital appreciation. That is where a lot of people lost their fortunes when the global financial crisis happened, and that is where I almost lost mine. When I was first building my portfolio in Australia, I was buying expensive properties, hoping that they were going to continue appreciating in value.

Did you catch that? I was *hoping*. What the hell?! HOPING is not a strategy! (I guess I didn't know what "buy low and sell high" meant back then.)

No one has a crystal ball. No one can predict the future. You do not know what is going to happen in the next 10 minutes. How can you possibly predict what will happen next year, or in five years, or in 10? You can't. It's impossible. So, you have to focus on the numbers that you have right now. The numbers today don't lie, and that's just *The Raw Truth*.

Back in 2005 and 2006, when the market was going through the roof, it was easy to lose sight of that. A lot of people on both the East Coast and the West Coast of the United States were getting greedy. They were buying expensive properties like crazy, thinking that those properties were just going to continue appreciating … that the real estate world was going to stay in fairy-tale "lala" butterfly-land forever. Even if that meant negative cash flow at the outset, the West Coasters reasoned, the capital appreciation would more than make up for their cash flow losses a few years down the road. Bad choice for them, as the road led straight to the edge of a very steep cliff. (Most investors got burned and are still trying to recover to this day.)

Sorry, mates. It just doesn't work like that. What goes up must come down and vice versa.

Take a cue from one of the shrewdest stock investors ever, Warren Buffett. "Be fearful when others are greedy, and greedy when others are fearful," he said. When people get greedy—like they did in the run-up to the housing downfall and Great Depression of 1927—the frenzy keeps pushing prices higher and higher until they can't be sustained anymore. And then everything comes tumbling down, like a house of cards in the wind.

So where are you if you've based your calculations on "appreciation" or the hope of appreciation at the mid- to peak point of a market cycle? It's just a risk that's not worth taking. And if the market did fall off the cliff just like it did so many times before, it could take decades to recover.

On the other hand, if you based your decisions on good, solid cash flow, you'll be sitting in a good position and most likely will be able to weather the storm with ease.

We live off cash flow, not capital appreciation and equity. Never forget that.

You can't put your hand in equity and go out and buy McDonald's. (Hypothetically, you could, and that would be called a HELOC: Home Equity Line of Credit. Using that money for personal stuff like McDonald's, etc., though, would be absolute suicide, in my opinion.) Conversely, you can put your hand in your account every single month because you're getting cash flow in the form of rent and use that money to go and buy a McDonald's or whatever else your heart desires. KFC maybe?

The whole idea of this thing called "real estate" is to generate enough money in cash flow from your investments each month that you can replace your corporate salary. And to grow that passive income source to give you the freedom so you can do what you want, where you want, and when you want.

Stick to Today's Numbers

It takes more than just hope to accomplish that. You've got to stay with reality. Today's reality. Today's numbers are real.

- What is the cost of the property?
- How much renovation does it need?
- How much are the taxes?
- How much is insurance going to cost?
- How much rental income will it produce?

If I could give you just one piece of advice to take away with you from this book, it would be this (and I can't stress it enough): While you are calculating all those numbers, always—*always!*—underestimate the income and overestimate the expenses. Give yourself a margin of safety just in case you made a mistake with your calculations. Because if you think it's not going to happen to you ... trust me, it will. It always does. Real estate is a rollercoaster of a ride with many highs and lows.

Then, once you have calculated all the numbers and you look at the end net cash flow yearly figure—and *if* that end net cash flow figure aligns with and gets you a step closer to your long-term end goal—that investment *might be* worth pursuing further. Any capital appreciation should just be considered the cherry on top—and never a major factor in your deal calculation process.

Now some of you may be thinking, "But, Engelo, what if the rents decline? I am looking at the numbers in the deal as they are today."

- I can buy the property for this much.
- I can renovate it for that much.
- These are my expenses.
- This is my income.
- This seems pretty easy, but what if the rents go down just like a property's value can?

Personally, I've never witnessed it happen. I've worked with investors who have been in the business their whole lives and have never seen rents decline either. Unless a nuclear power plant right next to your house blows up (you might as well kiss your butt goodbye then) or you are in a market that is heavily dependent on just one industry, like mining, for example. Overall, though, I just don't see it happening.

I'm going to go out on a very solid limb and say that rents will never decline. Along with food, shelter is the most basic of human necessities. People will always need a roof over their heads, so the demand will always be there. And inflation is always with us. As inflation goes up, rents also ultimately grow. Plus, the last I read was that we are all moving to Mars, so it seems like there isn't enough room left here. (Stop having 10 babies, people!) So, stay with today's numbers and you won't go wrong. You heard it here. From the Dingo himself!

Still, I know some of you can't help yourselves. (Probably all you folks who visit Vegas 14 times per year.) So, if you *are* going to speculate/gamble, there's a way to do it. Here's what I did:

A while back, I bought a property in an area right next to a hospital that I knew was expanding. I made the prediction that this hospital would continue to expand—and in the direction of where this property was located—so that one day its developers would come knocking on my door, offering to buy my house for a lot more than I paid for it. Sure enough, that's what happened.

But that's the only type of scenario where I think you should invest in real estate based on any capital growth projections. Maybe you have a strong hunch, or some inside information, or you are looking to invest in an area that has shown long-term historical growth. Maybe you're just a genius at market stats and trends. Or maybe you're just a witch (I hate cats, by the way). Any of those is a good indication that you might stumble across a market with potential for appreciation. But that area could just as easily tank and you could lose your shirt. Just remember: There's no such thing as a "sure thing."

And in any case, always, *always*, **always** base your investment decisions on the numbers in the deal as they are today. (Remember: The numbers don't lie.) If you're flipping, make sure the deal is profitable. If you're going to buy-renovate-rent, make sure that the cash flow aligns with your end goal and gets you a step closer to it.

Write this in big, bold, huge letters and put it where you will see it every day, multiple times a day:

Every single transaction must bring me a step closer to achieving my end goal. Every. Single. One. #Boom

One of my goals, for instance—and I have about 50 goals for each year—has always been to own a property in the Bahamas. From early on in my investing career, I have been working my tail off so that one day I could buy a waterfront property in the Bahamas. I dreamt of having established such a large cash-flowing portfolio that I can lay in the sun with my beautiful family by my side, sipping a cool, delightful pinã colada and watch my passive income pour in. And if I don't want to work and would rather jet off to another piece of paradise at a moment's notice, I can do that. Because the cash flow from my investments is real and predictable and provides financial freedom like no other strategy can.

By the way, I did buy my waterfront property in the Bahamas not too long ago. It doesn't look like much yet—we're just starting to build a little shack with stilts right on the beach. Fishing, anyone?

But the point is: I had an end goal clearly in mind (my Bahamas property is just one of many), and I pursued an investment strategy based on today's numbers that would generate the cash and cash flow to fulfill that dream.

I took the leap of faith, and I went out to chase my dream, not caring what anyone else was going to say. (And I can guarantee you, if I had listened, I would have heard a lot of skeptics and naysayers telling me I was crazy, and that it would never happen. To this day, and after I have proved them all wrong, some are still calling me crazy.) But you know what most of them are thinking now? "Wow! That guy's got moxie! He did exactly what I want to do except that I don't have the guts to try."

Those poor blokes are still slaving away at their mindless 9-to-5 jobs, chasing society's vision of the American Dream, but they're really just marching toward a regrettable end.

And me? Ha! I continue to hustle my butt off back in Toledo, Ohio, USA chasing more dreams—while renting a $700-a-month flat for me and my family, mind you—but I own a waterfront home in the Bahamas and in several other areas worldwide, like Croatia and Japan! How awesome is that?!

That's the power of cash flow, my friends. God bless the Queen! And long live the King!

"Begin with the end in mind."
— Stephen Covey

Chapter 5

LEVERAGE IS FOR PEASANTS

Psst! Wanna know the secret to getting rich in real estate without spending a penny of your own money?

Yeah? Well, so do I (haha)! But I've got news for you: It's not going to happen, mate!

Didn't we already go over this in Chapter 3? Yes, we did, but since it's so easy for a newbie or wannabe investor to get swindled back into that web of deceit, I'll repeat it again. Because I want you not just to hear those words in your head, but to etch them so deeply into your memory that you will never forget them. Otherwise, everything we're talking about in this book is a waste of your time and mine.

OK, then. Let's assume you fully ascribe to the mantra that money makes money—and making money takes money.

your mind, of knowing they've put their faith in you and are counting on you (and that you've got to pay them back—and extra, most likely), but now they think they have the right to put their own fingers in your business. A business they know zilch about.

Don't Expect Any Favors

Some of those family members or friends may have given you an interest-free or low-interest loan, but don't expect that from anybody else. With the institutional guys, you've got to fit into their neat little category and meet all their nonsensical requirements about credit scores, income, deal and location criteria, etc. And hard-money lenders will absolutely rob you all day long with their fees and terms.

Once everything is said and done, you've got no profit to take. It pretty much all goes to them. Even the more experienced "big boy" investors doing five to 10 flips per month are constantly complaining about hard money and how expensive and inconvenient it is.

When you borrow money—no matter whom you borrow it from—you don't have the freedom to do what you want, when you want and how you want to do it. There are just too many outside influences and stipulations that can jeopardize your real estate endeavors when you start your investing journey by immediately borrowing money.

SO DON'T DO IT! There's a time for leverage, but it's definitely *not* at the early stage of your journey.

Stop looking for the easy way out. All good things take time. Nothing comes easy in life. Stop being a lazy son-of-a-gun. Work hard. Work two jobs if you have to. Be frugal. Save the money and do your first certain amount of deals with all cash. As I've said before, you can start with $50,000 to $100,000, which is a lot of money to start investing in most of the markets in the U.S. and you will be well on the road to establishing yourself as a serious investor who knows what he or she is doing.

How to Get Started

Here's my advice:

Buy the cheapest, most run-down property you can. (Preferably one that just needs a cosmetic rehab.) Learn your trade on such properties, because the lower the amount of money you invest, the lower your risk is going to be. That's common sense. Don't do anything stupid like increasing the budget of money you put in for full-blown structural rehabs or to buy multifamily or commercial properties when you're just beginning. (Don't forget the KISS approach and don't get sucked into the B.S. that others are selling/spruiking you on.)

Start off small, with, say, a 2-bedroom, 1-bathroom home (under 1,000 square feet) that only needs a cosmetic rehab. Buy it, fix it and flip it as quickly as you can. (I know that it's easier said than done, but I'm not writing an investment thesis here, guys. Just the basics. Keep reading.) Get some numbers on the board. Rinse and repeat. Rinse and repeat. And make sure you are recording the details of everything as you go: Purchase price, rehab cost, sale price. Over and over, for every deal. Keep a spreadsheet. Take before-and-after photos. Do videos.

Once you prove without a doubt that you know how to flip for profit, then all of these other people—the spectators—will be falling all over themselves, begging to know who you are. They will want to be a part of your success, and they will come rushing to you, offering you an absolute boatload of money. Nowadays I get cold-pitched by lots of private lenders, banks and credit companies on a daily basis. They all come to the party just about when it's time to pop the champagne. Some of them have been great partners of mine, but most are not worth the time of day.

That, my friends, is the time when it's appropriate to use leverage. Then, and only then, should you use leverage, and you can use it to absolutely super-turbo-charge your efforts. Use leverage on *your* terms and nobody else's.

So remember: Prove yourself first (to yourself as well as to others) before you even think about going out and looking for leverage. You want to be the master of your fate, the captain of your soul. You do not want anyone controlling your destiny. The moment you start taking on leverage, you are not in control anymore.

That is why I emphasize that even when you are ready to go down this road—"Leverage Lane"—stay diversified and be patient. It takes at least five years, if not 10 or 15 to build a sustainable real estate portfolio, depending on how much time and effort you want to put into it. Nothing happens overnight.

If you want to play it safe, you should always build the foundation of your portfolio with cash-only properties. Your first three to five properties, depending on the market you're in, should be bought outright. (It will take you longer this way, but "slow and steady wins the marathon." Real estate investing isn't a sprint.)

How about that? Outright with cash. (I know what you're all thinking. My answer is: "Figure it out.") No loans. No mortgages. That way, you have that recurring income coming in every single month no matter what, which isn't costing you anything in mortgage repayments.

Here's When It's OK to Consider Leverage

Once you have that rock-solid foundation that no one can touch, that no one controls except for you, then you can start looking at leverage. Because heaven forbid, if something falls apart with half of your portfolio (there will be times where 30% of the properties you own in your portfolio will be experiencing vacancies all at the same time) because the global market tanks and everything has gone south, you will still have the foundation of your portfolio, which are those cash-owned properties producing cash flow every month that will help offset any other expenses on any leveraged properties you have. I've been sharing this same method for years now and with every investor with whom I come in contact.

Pity poor little you, if you're one of those investors who insisted on using high leverage for all—let's say 10—of your properties and then three to five of them become vacant. Guess what's going to happen? In order to cover those losses (maintenance, repairs, leasing fees, etc.), you are most likely going to have to dig deep into your own pocket and deplete the hard-earned money you made from your 9-to-5 job or any cash flow gained from your portfolio. Now, what if you lose that 9-to-5 job? Well, then you're really up a creek with no paddle. You declare bankruptcy like way too many investors did during the run-up to the global financial crisis.

Here's a sobering statistic: According to the American Bankruptcy Institute, total bankruptcy filings for the calendar year 2018 stood at 755,182. For the first half of 2019, there were 388,463 filings.

The possibility of debts outweighing assets is a rising risk, after years of low interest rates have lulled too many people back into leveraged spending.

What's the lesson here? All good things take time. Start with cash and build the foundation of your portfolio with cash. Forget about leverage until you really know what you're doing. Leverage is for peasants. Don't end up under a bridge. Control your own destiny.

There's no better way to do it.

"Every time you borrow money, you're robbing your future self."
— Nathan W. Morris

Chapter 6

TEAMWORK MAKES THE DREAM WORK

When you're considering where to do a deal or make an investment, what do you think is the most important, the most valuable, the single most crucial element to consider:

- The employment numbers?
- Population?
- Crime rate?
- Biggest employers?
- Capital growth projections?
- Vacancy statistics?

How can I put this? Nope. Not hardly. Not on your life. Not just no, but hell, no! No bloody way!!

You might as well base your decision on which direction the wind will be blowing or what the weather is going to be like in Madagascar for the next 30 days. Because none of those things is the main determinant of whether an investment deal is going to be a success. And yet, that's all I seem to hear.

I speak to a ton of investors on a daily basis, and I have spoken to more than 2,000 people in the last five years who have inquired about investing through my company or in my market. Investors from all over the country and all over the world: East Coast, West Coast, U.K., Canada, Australia, Asia, Madagascar (of all places, right?), Nigeria, you name it … (I wouldn't be surprised if someone from the Vatican called, also.)

And they all have one thing in common, and it drives me absolutely nuts: They all focus on the stats and demographics of a particular area.

Everybody's an Expert...

All these people think they are experts and have decided to hone in on Toledo, Ohio—or wherever else it might be—because they can do a quick Google search and study some hastily thrown-together reports from some data-collection company or new real estate tech start-up that has the magic formula. It's not hard to find whatever online stats you want to back up the point you're pushing … there are lots and lots of companies out there that track all of this and churn out their "exclusive" reports like clockwork, just so some investor halfway around the globe can call himself an expert on my backyard—or yours! As soon as you open your mind to the world of data and internet, in comes the trash. (Not all is trash, but most of it sure can be.)

All of those things are just out there to smudge your eyes and to sell reports. Without context, those numbers don't mean a thing. These companies run whatever data they run, but have they ever set foot in the local market where they're running that data? Heaven only knows how they even get their projections. In today's day and age, they say that "data" is like the new oil. I tend to agree, to a certain level. But it doesn't have much to do with the point that I'm proving here.

That's the wrong way to evaluate any area for investment. You are not an expert just because you can turn on a laptop and do a Google search. No out-of-towner is ever going to be able to buy a better property in my market than I can. No one will ever have his or her finger on the pulse of that market the way I do. And do you know why? Because I live it. I breathe it. I am here on the ground, in person, all day long, every single day, every week with my entire team, working the numbers. We are the ones making the numbers (data) that are used by all those online companies. How about that? (How do you like me now?)

We feel the market's heartbeat—every beat. We are the stats. We are the demographics. We understand the micro-economics of the market. My team and I—not a Google search. So stop basing your investment decisions on the stats and demographics of a particular area ... the capital growth projections ... the population growth ... yadda, yadda, yadda.

The number one thing that you need to do when you are starting your journey in real estate is to establish trust and strong relationships with the right people. Because those people are going to be your heart and soul, your eyes and ears on the ground, in a particular market, even if it's a market located in your own backyard. The people—not the stats and demographics—will make or break your investment. Business is easy. People make it difficult. And that's just *The Raw Truth*.

How do you know whom to surround yourself with? Well, first, consider the areas of expertise required to make you or your real estate investment venture successful. Even if you are skilled in some areas,

I'll wager you are less than good in others. Your team is going to need people in a number of areas, including realty, property management, construction, law, accounting, mentoring, title insurance, maintenance, mortgage lending, appraisal—and that's just for starters.

Your network equals your net worth. Never forget that. Together—with good trustworthy partners—your team is stronger and better.

As the Bible says in Ecclesiastes 4:9–12:

> *Two are better than one,*
> *because they have a good return for their labor:*
> *If either of them falls down,*
> *one can help the other up.*
> *But pity anyone who falls*
> *and has no one to help them up.*
> *Also, if two lie down together, they will keep warm.*
> *But how can one keep warm alone?*
> *Though one may be overpowered,*
> *two can defend themselves.*
> *A cord of three strands is not quickly broken.*

Another way I like to put it is this: Teamwork makes the dream work. But you've got to carefully choose those members of your team, because picking the wrong ones can turn your dream into a nightmare. You don't have to look far to find stories of partners cheating each other, or an employee embezzling thousands from a company. (This actually happened to me, when my property manager stole $7,000 in deposits from my tenants and my former office manager damaged the company to the tune of $250,000.)

This is proof that teamwork can either make the dream work—or turn it to a nightmare. You can buy the best house, in the best area, with the best capital growth projections and with the best cash flow, but if your property manager is incompetent or is a cheat, you're going to lose money. That property manager may misplace or steal your rent. All those stats and demographics have nothing to do with reality if the people aren't the right people. So forget about focusing on anything else except finding—and keeping—the right people on your team.

And on the other side of the spectrum, you could buy a house in the heart of the roughest ghetto with crime rates through the roof, where houses are falling apart and there is no capital growth and it seems like the world is going to end in that area—and you can still have a profitable investment. How? By wisely choosing and developing trust and a strong relationship with property managers who are legit, experienced, and who may have been born and raised in that market—or at the very least are intimately familiar with the community and the people in it. Sure (I say in jest), those property managers might have to collect rent wearing a bulletproof vest and driving a Hummer, but at least they are going to collect the rent, because they know how to influence those tenants and will deposit that money fairly in your account because they are trustworthy. And in return, creating a win-win-win for all involved parties: Tenant, landlord and property manager. (I used property managers as an example, but the same goes for other professions that are part of your team.)

I know people making millions and millions of dollars in the roughest ghettos of the country. Not because the numbers in that market make sense, but because the people they have selected in those markets make the numbers work.

Ground All Your Relationships in Trust

Now, let's go back to a very important point because I don't want to gloss over it. You better be careful and absolutely sure you can trust every single person you bring onto your team.

Believe me, it's easier than one might think to get suckered by a crooked operator who convinces you he's legit and trustworthy. People like that have cost me a lot of money over the years. So, I have come up with a magic question that you need to ask that will help identify those bad apples and toss them to the compost heap where they belong.

In this day and age, too many people are all about instant gratification. They want your money now. From the real estate agent, to the contractor, to the maintenance person, to the property manager ... they are not interested in taking the time and effort to build a solid, trust-based, long-term relationship. Instead, they are focused on "What can I get right now?"

Don't forget your end goal. It takes five, 10 or 15 years to reach the point of an established real estate investor who has hopefully achieved financial freedom. Delayed gratification is key here. Plant the seed now; reap the harvest later.

People who share this philosophy are the ones you should be looking to work with. For example: I would much rather make $10,000 a year over 10 years on multiple dealings with someone, than $50,000 on one transaction where I risk losing my reputation because my ill-chosen "team" members cut corners just to make a quick dime on a single deal.

And Now, for the Magic Question

Here it is: (drum roll, please...)

Are you willing to wait six, nine or 12 months to build trust and a strong relationship with me before we do any business together?

It's a simple question; ask it! You do not want to work with people who don't have any intention of getting to know you or understand your investment needs intimately. Tell them to go jump in the poo-poo-filled lake.

It's about delayed gratification. It's about the long-term vision and the bigger picture. You will eliminate 99.9% of shady operators with that question. They will stop responding to you (or you might hear something along the lines of, "But I don't want to miss out" or "Now is the perfect time.") They will not want to do business because they can't see dollar signs immediately when they look at you. Only the good ones will be willing to wait and be a part of your long-term vision without putting any pressure on you to "Hurry up!"

Now, even if you have found that hot deal where you want to jump into bed straightaway, still ask the question. See who will say yes. Not many will. But those who do are worth investigating further.

Here's one more thing to bear in mind before we move on: Don't lead people on if you don't have a genuine interest in working with them, as then they will tell *you* rightfully to go jump in the poo lake. I have had to do this more than I'd like.

Oh, and before we go to the next chapter, here is another quick Dingo tip: When interviewing prospective team members, make sure to Google their name and add the word "scam" behind it. (I told you I loved the internet, didn't I?)

You will be surprised at what you will find.

You're welcome!

"It takes a lifetime to build a reputation
and only five minutes to lose it."
— Warren Buffett

Chapter 7

NEGOTIATE LIKE A PIMP

As we've already established in a previous chapter, real estate is a numbers game. It comes down to doing this, on a daily basis—and I mean *each and every* single day:

- How many hours will you commit to working?
- How many emails will you send?
- How many phone calls will you make?
- How many meetings will you attend?
- How many social media posts will you compose?
- And how many offers will you submit?

That last one, mates, is absolutely huge!—for obvious reasons: You can't close a deal until you have found a property. And you can't buy a property until you make an offer!

That's the only way you're going to make the profit you need from each deal to put toward achieving your end goal. *Always* keep your end goal in mind!

So, hell yeah, it's a numbers game. And there's only one way to play it: by using the Dingo's patent-pending "throwing-mud-on-the-wall-until-something-sticks" method.

Actually, I have to credit my first-ever mentor with that. It was the first thing he ever taught me, and this is what he said: "The more mud you throw on the wall, eventually some will stick," meaning: Make low-ball offer after low-ball offer after low-ball offer, and eventually a desperate homeowner in distress will take you up on it. (I know what you're thinking, and I'll address your thoughts of my being an opportunistic devil later in this chapter.)

Don't expect it to be easy, though. When you come at those potential sellers with such ridiculously low offers, of course they're going to counter by slamming the door in your face first—and rightly so.

Stalk Your Market Like a Hawk

But listen to the Dingo and you'll still come out ahead. Here's what I want everyone to do: First of all, you need to familiarize yourself with a particular ZIP code, or neighborhood. You need to live and breathe that market. You need to know everyone who's doing anything in that market. From the real estate agents, to the buy-and-hold investors, to the buy-fix-and-flippers, to the wholesalers. I mean, you have to stalk that market like a hawk. Know what distressed properties are selling for, what renovated properties are selling for, what the rents are, how long it takes to sell a property ... everything and anything. Stalk the listing sites—Craigslist, Zillow, online auction sites, MLS and broker websites being the main ones. You can even ask Realtors what size underwear they wear when showing properties there. (OK, maybe not that one, but you get the point.)

Make that market yours and become an expert in it—love it, breathe it, own it, dream it! Once you understand what value (or a cheap property) means in that market, then you can start negotiating. And this is how you negotiate: You are going to be throwing as much mud on the wall as you possibly can.

Let me lay it all out for you as simply as I can. I'll make the numbers easy. (I'm really doing my best here with the simplicity; the exact numbers on a deal will always be more complex, so please keep that in mind.)

We now know the value of the market. We've studied it inside and out. We know everyone and everything. So, let's say, hypothetically, that we come across 100 properties on a weekly basis that are listed for an undervalued price compared to true market value.

Let's assume that after renovation—there is no such thing as a free lunch; you will have to renovate, some a bit more and others less—the value of each of those properties is $15. (I told you these numbers were going to be easy!) Right now, each property is listed for $10. Every one of them, because they are distressed. And remember: You don't make money buying a renovated product. You make money buying a *distressed asset*. So for each property, we are going to submit, in a very professional and diplomatic way, a $5 cash offer, with a quick close—as long as the title is clean and there aren't any back taxes or liens (you can even submit a "proof of funds" with your offer to show the seller how serious you are) on that property.

That's right. We are going to low-ball, as in throw mud on the wall. So, everyone, you better have really thick skin, because you are going to get a lot of heat for making such ludicrous offers. But if you want to make money in real estate, this is how you do it. Never forget: You make money when you buy, not when you sell. So, you have to buy dirt-cheap. And that's just *The Raw Truth*.

What Reaction Were You Expecting?

What do you think is going to happen? Most likely, the seller is going to react like this: "Are you freaking insane?! How dare you insult me with that offer?! Who do you think you are? You're a disgrace! Blah, blah, blah, blah, blah."

But, hey, you knew that was coming. You offered $5, and the seller wanted $10. That really is a pretty low offer. So that's going to happen probably 99 times out of 100 (make sure you've got your "grown-up pants" on). But that other time—that one time out of 100—you are going to stumble across a distressed seller who really, really needs out ... right now. He or she is going to come back to you and say, "Make that $7, and you have a deal." And you are going to go back to that seller, and you are going to say: "$6, and I'll take it." And that seller is most likely going to say, "OK; deal." (Sometimes there might be a bit more back and forth when negotiating, but always stay cool and level-headed. Never pay more than what your profit margin estimate allows.)

Just so you know, guys, I've done this more than 500 times, and I know it works. You just need to keep chipping away at submitting those offers.

So, you just bought a property for $6 that is going to be worth $15 once it's renovated. Remember, you've done your homework. You've studied that market (for months—if not a year) and you know how to renovate that property and how much it is going to cost you to do it. You have also established the right team and put them in place. So, you are going to spend another $3, let's say, renovating that house, which is going to put you in at a combined $9.

Now, let's make those numbers a bit more realistic. That property is actually going to cost you $90,000 (purchase and rehab—now you know why it is important to save that initial $50,000-$100,000 in cash before you start), but you are going to sell it for $150,000.

After closing costs, discounts, concessions, etc., you are going to get $130,000 net, showing a $40,000 net profit on investment. There's your annual paycheck right there. One helluva deal! Just because you're committed to the numbers and you threw enough mud on the wall, and you were willing to listen to the outrage that came back your way 99 times.

I know what you're probably thinking to yourself: "But Dingo, my market is too expensive, and those kinds of profits just don't work."

Well, thank you very much, but I have implemented the same strategy in various markets across the world, and it worked everywhere. The entry prices might be different, but the fundamentals of the strategy stay the same. So does the profit margin. Shoot for a minimum of 30%.

Now, if you really want to be a jerk about it and say, "The market I'm in just doesn't offer such a profit," then I suggest you move out of that market and look elsewhere.

You're welcome and congratulations.

Oh, I almost forgot: As I've mentioned before, when crunching the numbers on a deal like the above scenario, always underestimate the selling price and overestimate the rehab cost. Personally, I've never come in under budget on rehab. Just saying …

Shall We Continue Now?

You are going to do this every single day. You are going to submit offers every single day, all day long.

I can tell you right now that my team and I do this all day long, and we do hundreds of transactions like this every year. I don't necessarily make $40,000 a deal. I make less, because my market price point is lower (don't forget about that 30% profit margin), but this is truly how to negotiate: You throw mud on the wall and eventually some of it will stick.

So, imagine if you just do this once a year, you supplement your current income. If you do it twice, you double the average salary in the United States. If you do it four times, man, oh man, do you start to print some money. Sure does beat a day job…

Does this get you a step closer to achieving your end goal? Yes, it most certainly should! So have thick skin and negotiate like a pimp.

Now, don't forget this very important, very essential part of the equation:

When you do come across that one deal in 100 where a desperate seller agrees to your ridiculous low-ball offer, you had better have the cash in hand to make that deal happen. Because if you don't, you're a complete idiot who's messing with someone's life. That's why I say, save the freaking money! Make sure it's a good deal, also, so conduct enough due diligence in advance before pulling the trigger on your final offer. Make no mistakes.

Work hard. Be frugal. Forget about leverage, because you've only got a limited amount of time to close on these transactions. And leverage takes time. Too much time. There's no room for fooling around here. If the deal is too good to be true, you buy it straightaway, or someone else will. You don't wait. You know how long it's going to take you if you're looking to use leverage? God only knows. You probably won't even get the deal. That's why leverage sucks.

Keep the Emotion Out (I'm Not the Devil After All)

And here's another thing: Never, ever, ever base your investment decisions on emotion. Because if you start listening to little old Grandma whose husband just passed away or thinking about how much you love the look of the house and could see yourself living there, you're going to lose money. I know this, because it's happened to me many times over.

Yeah, I admit it. For all my tough talk and Raw Truth-telling, I'm a softy at heart. But your success (and your family's success) … your profit … depends on your taking all emotion out of any decision. You have to look at the cold, hard numbers in that deal, and those numbers need to make sense and suit your profit margin and end goal.

Hate it or love it, but this strategy will put you on top. I know this might sound terrible, mates, but business is business. Be firm but also be fair when submitting your low-ball offers.

Forget about the status of the sellers. It's not your fault that they've gotten themselves into such a big mess or whatever life has brought their way. It's their responsibility. If the shoe was on the other foot and you were in the quicksand instead of them, you know they'd be negotiating your butt down to the lowest bottom dollar they could get.

It's sad but true: It's a cruel world out there. It's eat or be eaten. Plus, the way I see it, you're offering a fantastic service: cash close, quick, no contingencies, etc. Much better than someone else looking to finance but pay more. We all know how difficult lenders are and how many times the loan falls through. Poor sellers then.

But when you do commit to performing on that transaction, you sure as hell better keep your word and close the deal, because that seller is depending on you. That seller never would have agreed to your low-ball offer unless he or she needed that cash—and right now. And I don't care if you made a big mistake and the deal won't be profitable. Honor your word, because that's all you've got. I've made many mistakes like this and bought stinkers because I overlooked something. I had to eat the loss (at least Grandma was happy).

So if you're going to throw mud at the wall, make sure you can back up your bluster with the cheese … the money … the green little soldiers.

One final note: Never, ever, ever bid against yourself. If a Realtor or seller comes back and says, "Highest and best by Monday," you tell him or her, "I wish the highest bidder all the best."

Do not pay even one dollar more for a property than what you should. Don't cry over a lost deal, either. There's always going to be another one around the corner. The opportunities are endless. There are many, many markets all around country—and the world. And if a deal doesn't work here, you can be sure it is going to work somewhere else.

Even out of principle, don't pay a penny more than you should. Because $1,000 more paid today on a small home could be $1 million in the future when you're doing a *huge* deal. Set the tone and stay true to your beliefs when you're a "nobody," because those guiding principles will really matter when the stakes get higher and you become a "somebody."

Remember: You make money when you buy, not when you sell. You must be willing to walk away from a deal at any given moment. No emotion. Cold as ice. If you can maintain that mindset, you will always win. That is negotiation at its finest.

> *"Great things are done by a series*
> *of small things brought together."*
> — Vincent Van Gogh

Chapter 8

BLOW WIND UP YOUR A$$

I'm a big believer in doing things differently. Not just for the sake of being contrary or just an obnoxious son-of-a-gun—although I've certainly been accused of that … but for a truly good reason: You're innovating, trailblazing, moving ahead of the pack because you've found a better way to do things and you want to get there first.

It's called leadership.

You want to be the rebel black sheep breaking off from that crowded, clueless herd that is mindlessly shuffling off toward the slaughterhouse. You want to stand out. Because that's what is going to get you noticed by others. People will start talking about you and they'll remember you. And as word gets out, more and more media and influencers will pick up on your story and spread it to an even bigger audience.

All of that is vital to helping your business endeavors succeed and grow, moving you closer—faster—toward your end goal. Remember: Achieving your end goal is what it's all about. And this book is about giving you many facets that can assist you on your journey toward realizing your dreams. And a very important facet when it comes to real estate—and any business, for that matter—is marketing.

But before you go rushing out half-cocked in the middle of traffic in just your skivvies—that'll get you noticed and get people talking about you, guaranteed (Yep; I kind of did that once)—you had better make darn sure you have your business plan well-thought-out and ready to roll.

Let me ask you:

- Do people know who you and your company are?
- Do they know what you do and specialize in?
- Do they know what your target customer looks like?
- Do people know what problems you can solve for them?

Your whole brand and marketing message need to revolve around answering those questions.

You need to make people's heads turn (in a good way!). You want them to sit up and take notice. But most important, you want them to remember you!

This is something I have been really, really, really good at. First of all, it's because of my crazy Australian accent, and my very aggressive, rude and passionate self, and the things that I say.

It's also because at my company, Ohio Cashflow, our messaging and branding is consistent, from our logo and colors to the markets we target, the investing strategies we implement and the principles we live by. No matter what platform we're talking about—Facebook, Twitter, Instagram, podcasts, radio, TV, newspapers, magazines, conferences, speaking engagements … whatever it is—we are consistent in what we say and how we say it.

Marketing 101

This isn't rocket science here, mates. If you want to stand out, and if you want to break new ground, you need to be an early adopter. You need to be that black sheep. You need to be the one to stir the pot in a particular market or industry niche, causing so much flavor that people "can smell what's cooking" a mile away.

Let me give you an example of how this works: Toledo, Ohio (not the biggest or sexiest city, by any means). Ohio Cashflow is the biggest single-family home buyer in Toledo. (We made the Inc. 5000 in 2018 and 2019.) Before we came here, no one knew anything about the Toledo market—or not much, anyway. But now, if someone mentions Toledo, for real estate purposes, they know Ohio Cashflow and Engelo Rumora. We made sure people remember us. And we put Toledo on the map for real estate investing.

How'd we do it? Among other things:

- We did our homework, and we knew Toledo had the right fundamentals in place for good deals with high cash flow and low competition
- We established our branding—Ohio Cashflow's name, slogan, logo design, colors, website, etc.
- We settled on our niche—none of this bouncing around so much that people are confused about what you do. Don't be a "jack of all trades but a master of none." Become a master in one specific thing and truly master it. We specialize in turnkey real estate investing. That's it.
- We wrote our backstory—the "about us" piece, company bio, mission statement, how we differ, elevator speech, our core values, how we can help others, etc.
- We paraded a flag with what our ideal client would look like and we would only cater to such individuals.

- We found people and other companies who share our beliefs and started working with them.
- And we concentrated on the numbers, pitching our company story—the same story—everywhere we could think of, over and over.

We got our story out. And it has snowballed ever since. We've been featured in magazines and newspaper articles, we regularly present at seminars, we do videos and guest radio/podcast interviews and TV shows. And best of all, we get a constant and consistent flow of new business every day.

Through it all, it goes without saying, we worked our tails off (and still do!) with a passion and purpose like you've never seen. And you can do the same. Just be different.

Now, I'm going to let you in on something really, truly awesome: I'm going to show you how to get publicity for free to help you get your own message out! (I'll gladly accept donations for my PR advice. Just mail a check to my office.)

The Best Publicity is Free Publicity

So, we'll assume you've got your company name, mission statement and the other basics settled, just like we mentioned a second ago.

The first important thing I advise you to do, especially in this day and age, is to get a website.

"But Engelo, I thought you were going to tell us how to do this for free. Those can cost thousands of dollars." Yeah, they can—if you want all those fancy bells and whistles and multiple pages with various opt-ins and custom-code B.S., etc. But we're talking about what you, as a beginning investor, need right now, when you are starting out.

All you need is a simple site—even just a single page—that establishes who you are and what you do. I'll be the first to tell you I am no tech-wizard, but even I was able to build my own website. I did it with Wix, which is one of a number of website-building plat-forms that offer a free version. (You can pay a small fee for hosting there, also.) Most of these have premade templates and easy instruc-tions. All it cost me and my team was our time. So, stop whining and just do it.

For all of you who already have a website, well done! Take the time now to review it and make it even better. If you haven't tweaked it in a while, you will be surprised by how many bugs it might have. Fix it!

Let me stress again how absolutely, vitally important it is for you to have a decent online presence. That is the first step to free publicity. People (media and other hosts/influencers) have to be able to find you, see you and know what you do.

There is absolutely no excuse for not being discoverable online. You've got to put yourself out there—everywhere—and tell your story, repeatedly. When you finally do start bringing in some serious money, it would be a good idea to hire a web developer and work closely with them to build you a full-blown, top-notch website. I sug-gest something "clean" and responsive, user-friendly, with a ton of eye-candy (opt-ins). The goal is to capture as many leads as possible and to get them on the phone. Feel free to copy what we have done with www.OhioCashflow.com. We have spent tens of thousands of dollars on web design and optimization. It works. You're welcome!

Now, how are you going to get discovered when you finally have your website? Social media. That's right. You're going to learn how to use social media (and not just for spying on other people's lives, but the right way), regardless of whether you can type or create video. I don't care if you can't type, because I'll tell you right now, I can't type—never could, never will. And I don't think I look good on camera or sound good on audio, but I still jumped into that pool of uncertainty and I have learned how to swim.

What are you doing on Facebook, Snapchat, Twitter, Instagram and Pinterest? Are you constantly asking people to be on their podcast or show? Are you pitching yourself to radio stations and television networks? Are you hustling event organizers to speak on their stage? Are you attending conferences and having booths there?

You need to be blowing wind up your backside nonstop. You need to be telling everyone who you are and what you do. You should be screaming at the top of your lungs telling the world how unique and different you are. Confidence backed by results and performance are beautiful things, my mates.

Compose a cold-pitch email and send it to the publisher of some publication you want to be featured in or to a host whose podcast you want to be interviewed on. I have said it before, and I'll say it again: Real estate is a numbers game, and so is this. The wider you cast the net with your cold-pitch email, the more media fish you will catch. And maybe even a whale.

Own Your Story

Be proud of who you are and of your story. I don't care if you were trimming trees while launching your real estate business at nights and on the weekends—it's your story and you should own it. Proudly share it with the world. Hell, I started out with nothing. When I went back to Australia after playing professional soccer, I had no job, and since I quit school at age 14, all I could find were dirty, manual-labor jobs until I saw what investing could do. That's a big part of my story and a lot of people can relate to it, as most of us work in dirty jobs that we don't like and want something better in life.

When you approach publishers, hosts or other journalists to pitch your story, that's one of the keys: Find a way to relate to them as individuals. Learn about their background, show interest in what they do and compliment their efforts or past stories they have written. And emphasize what you can do for them: "I want to be on your podcast not for my benefit, but for yours; I guarantee I will entertain and educate your audience."

Don't be selfish with a hidden agenda. People can see right through that. Be yourself and offer value. People buy people, and if they like you, they will buy into what you're saying.

Push yourself. Be polite but persistent. Even when I get rejected, I still follow up and show persistence. There was one editor I emailed who turned me down ... said my story didn't fit in with what they were looking to present to their audience. I said thanks, but did I forget them? No! A year later, after I had gotten some media coverage from a magazine, I emailed this editor again and said, "You may remember I approached you last year and my story didn't work then, but now take a look at this"—and I attached a PDF of that magazine article—"so what do you think about my story now?" This time, they were interested (lucky for them, because I would have started following up every quarter, then every month). People appreciate persistence. And don't be afraid to use previous media mention as leverage.

Find opportunities for public speaking. You can do this—even if you think you can't. (Public speaking is the biggest fear of mankind. Beat that and you beat anything.) Now, I'm not trained as a public speaker, nor do I have any intentions to ever sell from a stage. I'm very rude and raw in my presentations, but I tell it like it is and people appreciate it and you can bet they remember me for it!

I was told by an audience member at one of my presentations, "You tell people what they *should* hear, not what they want to hear." And that's the way I like to go about everything I do. It gets me noticed. And it gets me remembered.

And I'm also telling it like it is for all of you in this book. I promised you *The Raw Truth*, no matter what some might think or how much criticism I get. Even if it does end up being a national worst-seller.

You have probably seen a trend by now in my beliefs: Nothing comes easy, and all good things take commitment from a repetition standpoint, hard work and sacrifice.

I'm sorry to have to break it to you, mates, but even getting free publicity will come with its own set of obstacles and demands. Stop looking for an easy way because it just doesn't exist. You need to get that belief out of your system. Most things don't have a magic formula. Nothing beats hard work. Don't forget that.

When you are telling the world who you are and what you are doing, you have to stay consistent and persistent with your message. So, for example, if you portray your brand and your style in a very aggressive and passionate and rude and raw way like I do, don't transition from that. Stay passionate, stay rude, stay raw, stay energetic, stay aggressive. Always stay consistent with your message. Not everyone will like it or like you. But that's fine, because it's impossible to make everyone happy. Make sure to always do the right thing in all of your dealings with people, though.

Credibility is so important these days, when people can do a Google search and find out just about anything about anyone. It should go without saying: Stay true to your principles and don't do business with anyone using shady practices. You are whom you're with, so stick with legit folks only.

Principles matter, and people notice.

You can still be the black sheep—and you should be! Success comes from doing things differently. Stand out from the crowd. Think differently. Leave an impression. Do the right thing by others. And always stay true to yourself and your principles.

"You can have everything in life you want,
if you will just help other people get what they want."
— Zig Ziglar

Chapter 9

IT DOESN'T MATTER HOW BIG IT IS

I absolutely love this quote from the late motivational speaker Jim Rohn:

"There are two ways to have the tallest building in town. One is to tear everyone else's down, and the other is to build yours taller."

Which way would you go about it?

Sad to say, I have come across way too many people on my journey as a real estate investor and business owner who get a sick sense of satisfaction in tearing down others' accomplishments—and self-esteem—instead of making sure their own work is the best it can be.

That may get you ahead of everybody else for a time, but the path of destruction you leave in your wake is going to be noticed, I guarantee you. And your reputation for selfishness and conniving and cheating is eventually going to catch up with you and be your own deserved downfall. The world has a funny way of rewarding you for the good but also punishing you for the bad that you do. My advice to all such "yucky" people is to get that chip off your shoulder while you still have a chance.

Getting your jollies from seeing others fail is absolutely not the way to go. Trying to compare whose is bigger is just a stupid little-boys' game. We all have "our own clock," so it doesn't really matter who's at what time in their own journey's cycle. Keep your eyes on the prize—*your* prize, *your* end goal—not someone else's. Don't look down on people or companies that haven't reached your level. And certainly not just so you can lord it over them or use their status to build up your own.

If you do look down on others, though, you sure as hell better be willing to help them up.

Now, when I look at someone else, it's for inspiration and motivation. I look to successful companies and individuals to learn how they accomplished their goals and see if I can apply things they did to my own practice.

Hold on, there … did I just hear you call me a copycat?

Here's what I say to that: There's nothing wrong with that, as long as you copy the *right* cat—but add your own unique twist.

Why Reinvent the Wheel?

I'll gladly replicate the wheel that a successful business already has and I'll put it on my carriage so I can move as fast as they do (or maybe even faster). Those companies and individuals that are principled and credible will even help you change the tires! Because they want to help you succeed. They know that everyone's success is important for the industry to move forward and innovation to happen. They also know that there is enough business to go around for everyone. Plus, when you are the best, the competition doesn't matter. That's why you should always endeavor to be the best.

Now, if you really think that you're the next Mark Zuckerberg or

Steve Jobs, then go for it and invent the wheel. But for all you average Joe Blows out there like me: Stick to the basics of "copying the right cat."

That's one of the great things I love about this country. In the United States, people celebrate and look up to others who succeed, unlike in most other countries where the perception is that if you are successful, you only got there by screwing somebody else over. God bless America, because it truly is the best country in the world.

Unfortunately, just like with anything else, there will be some bad actors that have no problem knocking you down just so they can get ahead. You can spot some of them from a mile away, because they will clearly share their displeasure with you and what you're doing, but others can sneak up on you if you're not careful. They're all looking to knock your building down so theirs can be the tallest. So you've got to figure out what drives them and how you can steer clear of their wrecking balls.

First—and I hate to break this to you, but it's true—there are people out there who are going to hate you. Plain and simple, for whatever reason, they are going to hate how you look, talk, how you do business, and they would like nothing better than to see you fail. They make no secret of it. But the good news is that you see them coming and you will know what they are up to and what angle they are taking. No need to be scared of them.

But there are others that you *do* need to fear. They are the ones who have been taken over by the green-eyed monster: jealousy. You need to be very, very afraid; when others are jealous of you, they will do unimaginable things because they can't stand to see your success.

There's a Big Problem with Jealousy

Now, the problem with jealousy is there is no cure for it, because these people have created it from within themselves. You won't see these people until they are right on top of you. They are waiting patiently, plotting against you in the background for your failure. And when you fail, they will descend on you and kick you even further. I'm telling you: Watch out for these types! I have had these green-eyed monsters stalking my success ever since I started my entrepreneurial journey. Unfortunately, this just comes with the job of being the best. As you keep reaching higher and higher, they will always be lurking to cut you down.

As much as this might sound counterintuitive to you, when they do appear (trust me, you will know), it's better to confront them than to run away and hide. The trick is in *how* you confront them. Just suck it up, mates; do your best not to vomit and get in there and caress their personas and stroke their egos. (Yeah, I knew you wouldn't like it, but believe me, it does work.)

You have to put these folks on a pedestal. Put them above you. Even though deep down in your heart and soul you know you are bigger and better than they are—and you *are* bigger and better than they ever will be. But you have to praise them, flatter them—in a genuine way—and convince them that you look up to them at their level. (Yes, I know, it goes against your grain. But if you do not do this, you will have a green-eyed monster on your back—and that is not what you want, believe me.)

Bite your tongue. Put your own ego aside and caress and stroke theirs instead, because that is the only way these green-eyed monsters will leave you alone. As long as they think they are superior to you, they have no reason to waste their time on you. The last thing that you would want on your journey to the "Nirvana" of real estate riches would be to get into an "argy bargy" with one of these jealous beasts. The negative energy will occupy your thoughts, preventing you from focusing on getting bigger and better. Just let it be. My grandma said (translated from Croatian): "Jealous people are like fresh dog poo. If you poke poo with a stick, it stinks more. If you just let it be, eventually it turns white, becomes dust, and disintegrates into the ground."

It's literally true. Just remember poking dog poo with a stick when you were a kid.

So, folks, don't get caught up in all that ego-pumping nonsense.
Protect yourself. Mitigate risk.

Don't brag. Don't compare whose is biggest. Keep your head down.

Always strive to be bigger and better and let your actions speak louder than your words.

- Focus on your company.
- Focus on your journey.
- Focus on growing internally.
- Focus on growing externally.
- Be humble.

Look up to others who are more successful than you are. Replicate what they do. Love them for what they have achieved.

Only compete against yourself and become better than you where yesterday.

Associate yourself with the best, and you will become the best.

There are two quotes I especially like that help me stay focused on associating with the best. The first is another one from Jim Rohn: "You are the average of the five people you spend the most time with." Who are your five people?

And Henry Ford is widely credited with saying words to the effect that "I am smart enough to have smarter people around me doing the things that I can't do or don't wish to do."

That's why I always endeavor to surround myself with people who are positive and smarter than I am. I love being the dumbest person in the room. Because that means I'm doing things right.

And that is just *The Raw Truth*.

P.S. To my green-eyed monsters: "You fueled my success." Forever grateful, Dingo

"They hate me, 'cause they ain't me."
— Unknown

Chapter 10

TELL FAMILY AND FRIENDS TO SCREW OFF

Here's a message I have had to give—so many times that I've lost count—to well-meaning family and friends who continue to question my commitment to real estate investing:

Screw off!

Go away! Leave me alone!! And mind your own business!!!

Sounds quite harsh, doesn't it?

Now, don't get me wrong, I'm not suggesting you should do this in a vile or venom-filled way. Because, after all, they *do* think they have your best interests at heart. They do love you. But they just don't have a clue why we do what we do, or who or what we're doing it for.

So you have to ignore their noise!

Be prepared for the barrage and stay strong. Stick to your plan, because you, as a real estate investor and entrepreneur, are going to be misunderstood by nearly everyone for a very long time.

I told you earlier that your parents (and their parents, and theirs, etc., etc.) have been brainwashed into believing in that idiotic "American Dream." And they have tried their best to make you drink that same Kool-Aid.

Your whole life, Mummy and Daddy have been telling you that you need to go to college, you need to get a degree, you need to find a good-paying job, you need to get married, you need to buy a house, you need to have kids, blah, blah, blah. And now Mummy and Daddy are the ones telling you, "No, son; no, daughter—you shouldn't take $100,000 (that you have earned and saved, by the way) and go invest it in real estate. The market is about to tank. The economy seems weak. You don't know what you're doing. It's too risky. It's not as easy as those flipping shows portray it to be."

Unless your parents are economists working for a large investment bank, I would take all financial advice they give with a grain of salt. Even if they work in the field of finance, I'd still make my own decision if I were you.

The First Ones to Bring You Down

The first people who are going to bring you down are the ones closest to you. It's *The Raw Truth*.

Not your enemies. Not your haters. Not the people who are jealous of you. It's your very own family and friends. Why? Because you are starting to distance yourself from their stereotypical, stupid beliefs. They are the first ones (because they are closest to you) who are going to be in your ear telling you how risky it is, making you question yourself, "Is this worth it? Is this truly something that I want to be doing?

Do I really want to be disowned by my family?"

You're going to hear it so often you're going to get sick of it, I'm telling you. Even to this day my family is still in my ear: "Engelo, why are you working so hard? Why are you sacrificing so much? Why are you doing what you are doing? Slow down; you have lots of time." (OK, that one I kind of agree with; I'm only 31.) Get ready, folks, because the emotional drag is going to become almost unbearable.

So you need to "kindly" and "politely" tell everyone to leave you alone *and get out of your business*!

The sad part is that they don't even realize that you're doing it for them. They don't get it. They are still in chains. They are in the cage. They haven't broken free. They are still brainwashed by society and its beliefs are ingrained in them. It's a trap and they don't know any better.

Don't hate your family and friends for it. Love them for their innocence. Don't shove them totally out of your life. Don't even bother with trying to connect them to your entrepreneurial beliefs; just shut out their noise.

The drive behind your real estate endeavors should be for your family's and friends' benefit, first of all—not for your own, because it will help push you through the tough times. And get ready—because there are going to be many tough times ahead. You've got to love them for their concern, but don't pay attention to their dire warnings of doom and gloom.

There is a lot of garbage that gets said on a daily basis by a lot of people. It could be coming from your family, your friends, the news, social media … it could be coming from wherever. But one thing you simply must *not* do is let this nonstop, rapid-fire barrage of B.S. knock you down or push you off course. Because, believe me, you will regret it for the rest of your life. Decipher it all and be the judge of what you want to take on board and discard the rest.

Back in 2016, the American spoken-word artist, poet and filmmaker Prince Ea released a powerful video based on a hospital study in which 100 elderly patients, on the brink of death, shared their life's biggest regret. It wasn't anything that they had done that they most regretted, but rather the things they had left *un*done. "It is not death that most people are afraid of," Prince Ea says in the video. "It is getting to the end of life only to realize that you never truly lived."

Stay True to Your Course

The lesson is: Don't be afraid to take chances. Chart your own course to your dreams, and don't allow the noise from the naysayers around you to affect you, distract you or to become an emotional drag on you. Because if you get stuck on something a family member or friend (or anyone) has said—if you start fixating on that and questioning yourself—then you don't have your eye on the prize and you have lost before you even started. You are not focusing on the next deal, on your end goals, on your cash flow and on your dream.

What is your dream? What do you really want? Where do you want to be? Focus on these things only and on the folks truly supporting you in your endeavors.

I used to let it affect me, until I saw how utterly pointless it is to try to reason with somebody who's still stuck in their own ways (remember the saying, "You can't teach an old dog new tricks."). So, I do not care in the slightest what anyone else thinks. I know there are a lot of opinions contrary to mine out there; I just don't let those opinions affect me.

Notice I did *not* say you should deny them the chance to have their say. You do need to listen to everyone, because nuggets of wisdom come from the least-expected places at the least-expected times.

These opinions are going to come from a lot of different angles. They might come from a jealous angle. They might come from an "I'm worried about you" angle. They might come from an "I just really hate you" angle. Or they might come from someone's previous experience, or from others genuinely offering some awesome guidance.

The point is, you should take all of those opinions on board and evaluate them. It's actually very beneficial to talk to as many people as you can (your network equals your net worth), listen to as many different viewpoints as you can. Throw everything into the mix, stir it up, and the result is going to mold your decision for the better. Just don't let all these different viewpoints sway you while you're taking this all in. You—and no one else—have to have the final say.

When You Least Expect It...

Now, here's what I mean when I say that nuggets of wisdom come when you're least expecting them:

The best advice that I ever got was given to me by a drunk man in a rundown noodle bar in Sydney, Australia, many, many years ago. He had overheard a passionate conversation I was having, and he stopped me. He said, "You know, you remind me of someone very dear to me a long time ago..." I was thinking to myself, Where the hell is this going? But he continued talking and he said, "Never stop being like that because it will get you ahead in life." Hmmm, he got my attention with that one! He told me, "This is what my friend did, and you are the same. Fight for what you believe in, and only drop your guns when you are wrong, and then pick them straight up again." I'll never forget that. That's some of the best advice I've ever gotten—and it came from a drunk man in a rundown noodle bar in freaking Sydney, years ago! So that is proof, my mates, that you need to listen to everyone because sometimes, hidden in the bull, is some valuable advice or an "aha!" bit of truth that will open your eyes. So, spare the few minutes to listen, take the message on board and let that opinion mold you and your decisions for the better.

I know it's hard to tell the people who are closest to you to go you know where, but once again, as real estate investors and entrepreneurs, we must be willing to be misunderstood for a very, very long time. Even to this day, I am still misunderstood and people, including family and friends, don't understand why I do what I do. But I have learned to ignore the noise. And you need to, also.

If you get sucked into that argy-bargy, if you get sucked into that contrary opinion, if you get sucked into that nasty post on your social media, or nasty comment to a blog that you wrote, it all starts becoming an emotional drag on you. Don't let that mindless chatter start circulating in your mind, occupying your thought process and dragging you down. Because if you do, you are losing valuable time that you could be spending instead on creating, innovating and achieving your end goal.

Remember this: It's better to lose money than to lose time. Because when you lose money, you can get it back. But when you lose time, you can never get it back. Time is gone forever. And that is *The Raw Truth*.

Let the Naysayers Inspire You

So, don't allow your time to be wasted by obsessing about someone else's opinion, which could be worthy or it could be total nonsense. Don't take that chance. Evaluate that viewpoint quickly and move on. (No lingering.) Let it mold you, but don't let it get to you. Put your head down, work around the clock, let your actions speak louder than your words. Prove people wrong with your results.

My whole life, as I've said already, people have been telling me, "Engelo, you're not going to be a professional soccer player. You're not fast enough. Your lung capacity is not big enough. You just don't have the natural ability to succeed."

I was playing the game since I was 5 years old, and I became a professional soccer player when I was 18. That is the biggest achievement of my life to date. And I proudly have my professional jersey framed and hanging in my office.

Then, they have been telling me, "Engelo, you quit school at the age of 14. You can't type. You can't read. Your math is shocking. You can't have a successful business. You will never move to the United States and run a multimillion-dollar company."

You know what I say to that? I don't look too shabby on the front cover of that real estate magazine. And I'm running two multimillion-dollar companies—not just one. (Back-to-back years on the Inc. 5000 list. #booya)

And most recently, they said, "Engelo, you're not going to get on TV. You're too loud. You're too rude. You're not successful enough. You're not wealthy enough." Thanks to TLC for featuring us in their series of *This is Life Live* where we had the privilege of giving a house away to a family in need on live television. Not just once, but I have had numerous TV appearances due to our home give-away philanthropic efforts. I guess Crocodile Dundee did a good job in setting the path to TV "stardom" for all of us other Aussies.

So, don't let what others say affect you negatively. Let their words inspire you. Let the naysayers' doubts fuel your success. One day, you'll be needing to polish your backside really, really well because it is going to get a lot of kissing. All those same people will come back and beg to kiss it. So, make sure to polish it for them. I polish mine daily.

Kiss. Kiss.

P.S. What's next for me? Well, you know, just stuff like creating a billion-dollar company so I can give it all away after I buy my favorite sports team, AC Milan. I may run for mayor, for grins and giggles. Please doubt me, so I can prove you wrong, also.

P.S. #2 Tell your family that I said, "G'day."

P.S. #3 I might just go fishing instead...

*"Entrepreneurs must be willing to be misunderstood
for long periods of time."*
— Jeff Bezos

Chapter 11

MLS = MULTI-LEVEL SH**

Now, I'm sure you've heard of the MLS. ("The Holy Grail" for all good real estate deals … ummm, no!) Yes, of course, you have, as someone who's involved in buying and selling real estate—or who hopes to be. But I'm betting right now that your understanding of it— if we can even call it "understanding"—is totally off the mark.

This acronym gets thrown around so much that many people don't even know what those three letters stand for anymore. They just think, "Oh, the MLS—that's the be-all, end-all when it comes to finding the particulars on a property that's for sale." Everybody knows how valuable the MLS is, right? Because every real estate agent uses it, and you have to be a license-carrying member of their "elite real estate agent club" to even have access to it. If it weren't so valuable, it wouldn't be so exclusive, would it? Or at least, that's how the thinking goes.

But that's rubbish, mates!

MLS is supposed to stand for Multiple Listing Service, by the way. But in my opinion, it's simply more of that nonsense that everyone believes in: that the MLS is the best and easiest way to find deals. I'm here to tell you that you don't need the MLS or a real estate agent to find good deals.

The MLS is the first place every Bob or Betty and their dog looks for deals after they've been watching a TV flipping show, or reading an article, or taking some guru's course. Why? Because it's by far the easiest, and of course no one wants to do any work these days. Everyone wants something for nothing!

But understand this: If you want to succeed, you can't be like everyone else.

And the MLS is the sole place where all of those amazing licensed Realtors point you, because that is the only platform where an amazing licensed Realtor gets a commission. Many of them don't want to work hard, either (God forbid finding you an off-market pocket listing); they want something for nothing. Everyone wants something for nothing these days!

Realtors like the MLS because there are so many eyes on it and because it increases competition. They can't lose and will get paid, no matter what. But let me fill you in on something: Wherever you have the most eyes is *not* where you're going to find the best bargains. *Period*! That's *The Raw Truth*.

As I've already said in a prior chapter, if a Realtor comes back to you and says, "highest and best" after your most recent offer, you should always answer, "I wish the highest bidder all the best." There is always going to be another deal out there, so don't cry over a missed opportunity. Never, ever get into any bidding wars or long, drawn-out negotiations, as it's just not worth it. That's just a way for them to run up the price and get themselves a fatter commission check. Stick to your strategy, don't bid against yourself, and walk away until another opportunity comes along.

There's a Better Place to Start

Thanks, but no thanks. The MLS is the last place that you should look for deals, not the first place—like it is for so many investors. I don't care what any Realtor or real estate agent tells you, or any guru, or any book you've read, or any blog. I know a better way to find deals—or several, actually.

Here you go:

- Yellow-letter campaigns
- Craigslist
- And there are others, also, like wholesalers and birddogs, auction websites, FSBOs (for sale by owner), etc.

Hands down, though, yellow-letter campaigns are the best way to find deals. Here's how to do it: First, you identify a likely area (one that has potential due to gentrification or new infrastructure being built). Then you want to find out what properties are owned by people who would be likely to agree to a discounted price if it could get them a quick sale. You can check the county records to find absentee homeowners, as these folks are the most likely to sell at a discount. You can also browse for homeowners who have been living in the same home for more than 20 years. (In Ohio, for example, folks like to downsize and retire to Florida so they are always looking to sell quickly and cheaply. Note: Every state is different and so is the available information on the various county record sites.) Or you can pick out houses in disrepair or rundown condition just by driving through the neighborhoods. That can be a sign of an owner in financial distress or maybe someone who just doesn't want to take care of the maintenance anymore and who would welcome a way out from under that burden.

And Why is it Called That, Anyway?

So you're going to send out a "yellow letter" to these home-owners (you can find these people's names and mailing details via the county records site) that looks handwritten, and it's going to say something like this:

"Hi (homeowner), my name is Engelo, and I just rode my bicycle past your house at 1234 XYZ Street. I am looking at moving into the area. I am interested in buying your home. I am a cash buyer and can buy your home very quickly. Give me a call."

There are many different letter templates and designs. I suggest testing some of them out to see which works best for your chosen area.

(The reason this tactic is called a "yellow-letter" is because, back in the day, these actually were handwritten notes, often on yellow legal paper.)

Now, if you're only looking at doing a few deals per year, then you can do this all by yourself, just like in the good old days. Be very diligent, though, when identifying prospect properties so that your manual efforts don't go to waste. But if you want to be a true *boss* and send out thousands and thousands of yellow letters via an actual cam-paign, I suggest you hire an online lead generation mailing company that can do all of this for you.

Once the mailings are sent (I'm assuming that you're a boss), you are going to wait for the calls to start pouring in. You are going to pick up the calls or call back if you missed them (make sure your voicemail is set up explaining who you are and what you do). You are then going to negotiate! In a similar way to how I explained in Chapter 7, I have composed a free step-by-step guide which you can download on my website, www.EngeloRumora.com. BEWARE (shameless plug alert): You can also pay me a fortune for my consulting, and then you'll really have the edge on finding bargain deals. #boom

Now, granted, this strategy is going to take you the most amount of time and expense, but hey, nothing comes easy. Haven't we already established that you need to work your butt off to be successful?

By the way, I send out thousands and thousands of yellow-letter campaigns on a monthly basis, so I know what I'm talking about when I say it's a lot of work. But they also are going to give you the best bang for your buck, by far.

Just recently, I bought a 4-bedroom, 2-bath brick house on a corner lot for $23,000 (yep, God bless Ohio!) that I wholesaled (more on wholesaling in the next chapter) to someone else for $53,000. After rehab the value would have been around $120,000. A great win/win for me and the investor looking to flip. Another deal that I did not too long ago was a 2-bedroom, 1-bath brick property that fronted a golf course. I bought this one for $20,000 (yep again, God bless Ohio) and converted it into a 3-bedroom, 1.5-bath for $30,000 in rehab costs. After selling it for $119,000 I made a tidy $50,000 net profit. Not bad for two months' worth of work. Just another day in the office, mates, and you can do the same deals using the yellow-letter campaign strategy. I invite you to check out the Midwest. It's just a fantastic, blue-collar cash flow market.

When you're starting off, you're probably going to have to do a lot of the work yourself, but after you get some momentum (and cash flow) going, you can look into a customized CRM system with processes that will allow you to put this on auto-pilot. For instance, you can integrate with a VA (virtual assistant) service so the calls will be going to them rather than directly to your cell phone. That's a huge time-saver! But wait until you can afford all of those gadgets and extra expenses. Start off small, keep your costs to a minimum, and drive those sales and that revenue.

The Next-Best Tactic

Another platform that you can use to find great bargains is Craigslist. A few years ago, I bought 36 properties on Craigslist in just that year! Yes, 36 properties off bloody Craigslist. There's a reason these strategies—yellow letter campaigns and Craigslist—are such gold mines for finding bargain properties. Most of these people are uninformed about selling real estate. They've got the ridiculous idea in their heads that they are going to save money by not listing their property with a real estate agent. (As annoyed as I can get with some of them, most Realtors are very good with understanding markets and fair property values.) These DIY sellers think they're outsmarting everyone by going the rogue route, by selling the property to you because of a little letter you sent them, or by listing their home on Craigslist, hoping someone is going to see their ad and buy. They may think they're in the driver's seat, but they're not; you are. And you should capitalize on their mistake.

Be firm but fair. Always look for the win-win (not just in real estate, but in all facets of life). But ultimately, understand that you are working with unsophisticated sellers whose situation presents you this great bargain because they need a quick sale. Or they need a cash buyer because the condition of their property doesn't meet the requirements for someone to buy it with traditional financing.

Now, there's work involved with Craigslist, too. You have to stalk/ refresh Craigslist on a daily basis. I used to refresh the tab three to five times a day. I knew my market. I knew the value. I knew the numbers. When an opportunity presented itself, I would call the ad number straightaway and go see the house that day, and I would be closing on it five days later. Time is of the essence when it comes to finding great deals and buying properties cheap. And so is having the cash handy to do so.

One thing that can be another major benefit to you is the depth of your bench—that is, the other players on your team. You will find me repeating this over and over again: "Your network equals your net worth." Build relationships with wholesalers, birddogs and others who can bring deals to you. Network, network, network—every day! Explain your criteria to them and get them to slowly start sending you the deals they find. Once you prove yourself by performing on something they send you, the wholesalers and birddogs will absolutely flood you with new inventory they have. Institutional buyers and hedge funds, too, might have some exclusive pocket listings that they bought in bulk and are looking to liquidate "one-offs."

The MLS can't hold a candle to any of these strategies, because the good deals just aren't on there.

The MLS is Good for Something, After All

Now, having done a pretty awesome job of bashing the MLS and showing you why you shouldn't dedicate much time to it, I will acknowledge that it does have one redeeming quality. If you can somehow get access to it (get your real estate license or work with a super-investor-friendly real estate agent), the MLS can be useful in confirming the accuracy of all the findings you've made via other platforms.

On the MLS, you can run a variety of reports (like a CMA—Comparative Market Analysis), check out comparable sales and listing histories, days on market, find agent and broker info and other useful stats/information. But I repeat: Never solely rely on the MLS for doing your research on a market or a property within a given market. And to be completely honest, you don't need it, anyway! I only recently learned how to use the MLS after acquiring a real estate brokerage. I had already done around 400 deals without having access to or literally buying any property off the MLS.

Here's my advice: Become an expert and network enough in your own market and then the MLS won't matter. When you have studied your market inside and out and can feel the pulse of that market on a daily basis, you won't need to look up all these comparable sales or study any reports. You'll already know what the numbers are by heart.

For example: Let's say I've been scanning Craigslist and I come across an ad for a 2-bedroom, 1-bath house on a particular street in a particular neighborhood in Toledo, Ohio, and it's listed for, say, $27,000. Because I have become an expert in my market, I immediately can picture in my head the neighborhood where that property is located. (It will take years and countless deals to gain that experience so don't feel ashamed to do a quick Google street-view search or call a more experienced investor to ask them for advice. Practice makes perfect, so keep underwriting as many deals as possible every day.) And I also know the value of the surrounding homes in that area and their basic structure (in terms of number of bedrooms and bathrooms, as well as square footage). So, I will have a pretty good sense of whether that is underpriced or overpriced for that neighborhood and what kind of owners or tenants are drawn to that area. Knowing all that, I can either pass on that opportunity, or follow up with a call to the sellers and an in-person visit. Believe me, it's so much more efficient if you don't have to waste time calling on each and every possible great opportunity you find. This way, I can skip over the duds and devote more of my time and effort to the deals that are ultimately going to make me money. (Give it time and repetition and you will get there also.)

And there are plenty of other resources out there, to help you gauge the worthiness of any given deal. If you need information about previous sales history, liens, back taxes and more in-depth details on the properties' characteristics, do a search of the county records or enlist your trusted title company to do research for you for a small fee.

MLS? Who needs the MLS? Certainly not me. And you don't, either. So, don't you dare use "not having access to the MLS" as an excuse for not finding great deals. They are out there. You just need to look under every rock. Make sure to check your pockets. There might be one hiding there, also…

*"Ask and it will be given to you; seek and you will find;
knock and the door will be opened to you."*
— Matthew 7:7

Chapter 12

WHOLESALING IS "ILLEGAL"

I swear, I feel like a broken record sometimes, having to say it over and over—yet again—that you have to have money to make money. It's the same when it comes to wholesaling, just as it is with every other aspect or strategy of real estate investing. And all this talk about how to "make money with no money" is pure B.S. artwork put together by a broke real estate blogger—or even worse, a wannabe coach or mentor "guru." Whenever someone tells you that "it's easy and simple" to make money in real estate, run!

It really chafes me to think about how many investors out there are falling for this garbage ... these stupid "you don't need money" schemes. Not only is it just fundamentally unsound, but I also personally find it unethical and reprehensible—even if wholesaling is not technically "illegal" where you are. And we'll get back to that point in a minute. But first let me explain why I find the practice of wholesaling so disgusting, with this example:

So, you've decided to be a wholesaler. You've gone out and found little old Grandma, who has agreed to sell you her house for $30,000. You don't have the cash, but she doesn't know that; she thinks you *do* have the cash, because that's the lie you told her. (Good one, Mr. Unethical…)

Here's your plan: Once little old Grandma commits to signing that contract, you're going to go out and list that property for $49,000 on Craigslist or Facebook, email your junk buyers list (takes years to build, mate, just as an FYI) or focus on some other place that some lowlife jerk advised you to do, with the hope that a cash buyer is going to come along and buy that property from you for $49,000. Then you will assign the contract to that cash buyer. Little old Grandma gets her $30,000 and you get to pocket the $19,000 difference. Pretty sweet, don't you think? And oh, so very easy! Or is it?

It's a scenario that all those wholesaling gurus out there paint for would-be investors all the time, brainwashing so many otherwise-smart people into thinking you can pull this off without using *any* of your own money. Just find a willing seller and a qualified cash buyer who's going to perform … how hard could that be?

Well, unfortunately, it doesn't really work out like that.

Don't Believe the Hype

Don't you dare listen to those gurus and bloggers who claim to be able to teach you to make money with "no money." It's sad seeing how many folks fall for it. Don't be a sucker.

I said it before, I'll say it now, and I'm sure I'll say it again—several times—before we're done: You might as well stop reading this book unless you are willing to have $50,000 to $100,000 in hand before you go looking for little old Grandma and her house to buy. Don't even attempt to invest in real estate if you don't have that money available—*in cash*! You might as well throw this book straight in the trash. (Well, I'd prefer you give it away to someone who might find it useful.) Honestly, you might as well, because unless you have the money, you're not going to achieve anything significant. It is just not going to work, in my opinion, and all of my advice in this book will be pointless. Prove to yourself and to me that you can work hard, live a frugal life and save a minimum of $50,000.

Think of that $50,000 to $100,000 this way: It is the basic foundation of your investing "house." You need something in place that you can build on in your investing journey. You can't hope to do any successful deals without a foundation of cash any more than you can expect to build a strong house by shoving a bunch of 2x4s in the sand. It's just all going to come tumbling down around you, believe me. That's *The Raw Truth*.

Not to mention, wholesaling isn't even legal in all states. A lot of states have laws that say you cannot market a property for sale if you do not legally own it (or if you don't have a real estate license). Meaning you have to pay little old Grandma her $30,000 *before* you can advertise it for sale to someone else for $49,000 and then pocket the $19,000 difference. If it's such a stellar deal (like it should be if you know what you're doing) then you should have no issues with buying the property outright, anyway. Not having "skin in the game" allows folks to be loose and reckless with their acquisition criteria.

Of course, many people have gotten around that by means of a highly paid attorney and the excuse that "Judge, Your Honor, Mr. Division of Real Estate investigator, I always intended to buy it first, but then my circumstances changed, so I had to assign the contract to someone else, blah, blah, blah." Give me a break with that mumbo jumbo and just do the right thing. Do good, and "good" will come back around. Plus, if you have a conscience (like me) you'll want to sleep in peace at night.

But I'm not here to debate the finer details of this argument. The point to this chapter is to make sure that if you do pursue wholesaling, you do it the right way. Morally as well as legally. Here's what I mean by that:

When you get little old Grandma to sell you her house for $30,000, have the cash in your account so you can close on that transaction. If you can't wholesale it within a month because you can't find a buyer for whatever reason, you buy the house yourself! (Your genuine intention always needs to be to buy, and why not, if the deal is stellar, just like I mentioned above.) Don't let little old Grandma down. Little old Grandma is depending upon you to purchase the house. She wouldn't be selling if she didn't have some need or plan for the money. And she has trusted you when you promised her you would buy it from her by a certain date or whatever cockamamie story you told her.

What's Your Reputation Worth?

Your credibility is on the line. As is your character. So be a player. Put skin in the game. Put your money where your mouth is. If it's really the super-awesome deal you told little old Grandma it was, then you close that transaction yourself if you haven't lined up a buyer by closing. *Then* you can go wholesale it or even "wholetail" it. Or fix it and flip it. (You make great money—sometimes a lot more—by fixing-and-flipping a property. More on that in the next chapter.) If you don't want to do that—and if the deal *is* really good—then simply continue marketing it. Wait for someone to come along and buy it from you, and *then* you make your $19,000 profit or whatever it comes out to after all that. (Try reducing the price if you're not getting many hits and refreshing your marketing ads. New headings, new content, new photos, etc.)

There is nothing worse in this industry than investors who get little old Grandma's hopes up and then don't come through with the deal they promised. You can only do that so many times before you lose your reputation. It's a small world out there. If you start doing stupid stuff like that, you will lose your reputation, and your own real estate dreams will go bye-bye.

Now listen, mates. I know I'm coming on strong here, but that's the purpose of this book and it's because I have your best interests in mind. I have made my own share of mistakes and I want to spare you that pain. And safeguard your reputation.

I haven't ever left any little old Grandmas (or any other seller) high and dry, but I have made mistakes in committing to buy properties that I did not thoroughly inspect. They were bad deals that I knew were going to cost me—not make me—a lot of money. A boatload of money! But I didn't back out of those deals. I closed on the transactions knowing I was going to lose money because I had committed to the sellers. I was a cash buyer. I told the sellers I would close quickly, and it wasn't their fault that I didn't inspect the properties thoroughly or negotiate a better price. So, I still closed on the deals, because once again, you don't want to lose your reputation. You want to come through on your word. And you want to sleep in peace at night, knowing you're a sound real estate investor.

Your word is what matters. To hell with contracts! A "gentlemen's agreement," a handshake, looking someone in the eye and telling that person, "I will do this" should be sufficient enough. That's the way I like to do business, my mates. Think about your morals. I also encourage you to Google my name and try finding any dirt on me. Not just my name, but any one of my companies. The dirt just doesn't exist, as we always honor our word and do our best. Be the same and do the same, mates. Your name and your word are all you've got.

So, before you delve into wholesaling in your state, of course make sure it is legal there and that the Division of Real Estate won't give you a hard time. And then, do it the right way.

Have the cash in your account.

Don't let people down and risk losing your reputation.

Don't believe in these programs and courses that make it look easy. Nothing comes easy in life.

Granted, there are some good wholesalers who are doing hundreds of deals per year and who make it *look* easy. But keep in mind, too, that it took them years to get there and they've got the capital—their "foundation" of cash. This allows them to back any deal that doesn't come through and close on it themselves if need be and not scar their reputations.

So, heed my broken record, because it's going to keep playing on … and on … and on, like your favorite tune: Don't think you can make money without first having money. You just can't.

Oh, I almost forgot. Little old Grandma's name is "Karma," and she can come back to bite you big-time.

"In any moment of decision, the best thing you can do is the right thing, the next best thing is the wrong thing, and the worst thing you can do is nothing."
— Theodore Roosevelt

Chapter 13

FLIP LIKE A PORN STAR

Fix-and-flip is the current "sexy" thing to do in real estate investing, right? Just look at all those TV flipping shows with all those puffed-up investors in their $5,000 suits, fake nails and Rolex watches, picking out $12,000 bathtubs (while at the same time slinging a sledgehammer)…

What the hell?! Don't you dare believe that! That is the most ridiculous garbage that I have ever heard or seen in my life. There is nothing sexy about making money in real estate. It's not supposed to be sexy. In fact, it's supposed to be downright ugly. As in: Gritty. Repetitious. Boring! That's *The Raw Truth*.

You know how ugly and boring it should be? So ugly and boring that you don't even need to do anything. (The better you get, the more boring it becomes.) Once you've really mastered this, you don't even need to see the house. You can shuffle paperwork and make millions and millions of dollars from the comfort of your office or your home or a coffee shop or a tiki bar in the Bahamas (my preference). You don't even need to go and pick up a hammer. Sounds pretty lame, doesn't it? Well, let me tell you something that doesn't.

I know investors right now who are doing 200 to 300 deals a year and don't even go on site to look at the property. They shuffle paper. There is nothing sexy about that. But I'll tell you what *is* sexy and exciting: That big, fat balance in their bank accounts. Now, that's truly sexy!!

The whole point in any real estate investing strategy is to make money—and to make it as fast as you can. That starts with becoming a master at finding and buying properties —the *right* properties in the right market—dirt cheap. Be patient and wait for the right deal to come along in the right area that you can buy for the right price that needs the right amount of rehab work.

In flipping, a good rule of thumb is this: You always want to renovate your house better than any other comparable sale property on that street or in that area but list it slightly cheaper than any of the others. Why? Because time is money. You want to get "in and out" as quickly as possible so you can move on to the next one. (Just like a porn star.)

No Need to Get Greedy

You do not have to ask for top dollar. Don't hold out for months for a few extra dollars. Hit the sweet spot with your listing price and you'll have buyers lining up to submit offers within 48 hours of the listing going live. Remember, your overall annual profit is dependent on volume. The more deals that you can do every single year, the better. Yes, there will be the occasional "whale" property that will deliver a fat profit, but I suggest you focus on keeping deals turning over more consistently for smaller chunks of money. It's better to make less money consistently than "more" on the occasional deal only.

So, what's the secret? That's the great thing, mates ... there really is no top-secret, magic formula for this (just like there isn't for other stuff). It's common sense. But there are some general guidelines that you need to keep in mind and follow.

My advice is to start small. Sharpen your teeth on a very simple cosmetic renovation. As I've said before, you make money when you buy—not when you sell.

So, you not only want to buy cheap, you also want to limit the amount of money you put into the project. (Less capital invested equals less risk.) Definitely don't get caught up in any structural rehabs; that will eat up both your money and time faster than you can imagine. The more renovation a property needs, the more money you will have to invest, the longer your time frame is going to be and the higher the risk of something going wrong (like a contractor disappearing or the city shutting down the job). Speaking of which: You *will* incur extra expense for unexpected repairs or sometimes from mistakes during the rehab process. So, buying dirt cheap will give you a margin of safety to absorb the budget blowout and still make a profit on the back end. (And I bet my house in the Bahamas that you will go over budget on almost every rehab. I do.)

Now, I'm not saying you should look for the most rundown, structurally impaired, dirt-cheap and ugly house on the block just because it is priced way lower than everything else. You want to find a house that is of similar style to others in the neighborhood in size and build. Study what other successful investors are doing and what kind of improvements they're making. Don't go overboard on upgrades by overcapitalizing unnecessarily. Aim instead for that sweet spot so your property is just a cut above other renovated products, but you can sell it quicker for a tiny bit less and still make a good profit. For example: Do most of the other comparable sales have basic white appliances? Then make yours stainless steel (or at least "look-alike" stainless steel).

Another reason for focusing on cosmetic rather than structural rehabs is so you can maintain control over your project. Once you move past things like simple repainting, carpet installs, mini kitchen and bathroom overhauls—when you get into structural renovations, add-ons, subdivisions or new construction—then you've entered a whole different world (a world that I don't play in and neither should you if you're investing in the right market). At that point, you have to start asking for permits and you increasingly become subject to outside influences like lenders, or city regulators, or an architect, or an expensive licensed contractor or whoever it may be. And when you lose control to those outside forces, that's when you can start losing money, too.

Always strive to be the master of your fate and the captain of your soul by controlling as much as you can and by solely calling all of the shots. The more moving parts you have, the higher the chances of something going wrong with one of them.

Next tip: Keep yourself out of the equation! By that, I mean, don't go into a potential deal thinking, "Hmmm, what would it take for me to want to live here?" You've got to be off your freaking chops with such a "rookie" thought process! Picturing yourself living in that home has nothing to do with the profitability of the transaction. What the hell are you thinking? That's insanity! STOP!

Never, ever go into a deal imagining how you would fix up the property to suit your own needs and style of living. The person you need to be concerned with is the ultimate buyer for that property. Educate yourself on the target demographic. What do those people want in a home? What is their income? What mortgage payment can they afford? Cater your renovations to them and their wants/needs. Just because you want a pool doesn't mean that buyers in that area want a pool, for instance. Maybe a pool is too expensive to maintain in the winter, like it is here in Ohio. The point is, this isn't about you and what you want. Put yourself in the shoes of that prospect who will one day be buying your property. You can't go wrong by taking an in-depth dive into every comparable home that sold within the last six months and is located half a mile or less from yours. This is your golden ticket to figuring out the local homebuyer profiles.

Master One Strategy at a Time

And finally, do yourself and me a favor: Stay with single-family residences until you know that strategy inside and out. Do deal after deal, year after year, until it becomes so boring that you doze off and can do it in your sleep. Then, and only then, can you think about doing multifamily, or commercial, hotels, strip malls or new-builds. I've done more than 1,000 (I stopped counting at deal #1,000) real estate deals and have only recently started looking into commercial and multifamily. So, don't call me saying you're a beginner and asking for advice on a commercial rehab, because I'll tell you to go jump in the nearest poo-poo river. Start slow and small and build from there.

"Real estate investing isn't meant to be 'pretty.'
It's supposed to be 'profitable.'"
— Engelo Rumora

Chapter 14

GET MARRIED WHEN YOU'RE LOADED

Let's back up a bit and review the things I've been hammering on up to this point. (They say that in order to remember something, you need to hear or repeat it seven times.)

First: You have to have money to make money. As I hope I have made abundantly crystal-clear by now, you need to have saved $50,000 to $100,000—in cash—*before* you invest in anything.

Just as important: Make absolutely certain that when you *do* start investing, every deal moves you a step closer to your end goal. That's what real estate investing is all about.

In our case, we have created a hypothetical end goal (see Chapter 3) that 10 years down the road, we want to be earning $10,000 a month in passive income, or $120,000 a year. Assuming a 10% return, we need to have $1.2 million—in cold hard cash—invested in cash-flowing properties. Pretty straight-forward…

How to Get There From Here

So how are we going to get from here ($50,000-$100,000) to there ($1.2 million)?

Not by doing a single deal, that's for sure. Unless you strike oil underneath that fixer-upper you just bought with your $50,000-$100,000—not a likely scenario.

The reality is that real estate is a long-term game. It's not a one-night stand. It's a marriage. You don't just take your $50,000-$100,000 and buy, renovate and sell a property and expect to pull out a cool $1.2 million in profit from that one, single transaction. Leave that kind of stuff to the magicians like David Blaine and David Copperfield. (Well, I guess if your name is David, you might be able to pull off a deal like that also.)

Slow and Steady as She Goes

You ultimately get to your end goal one deal at a time, earning profit each time, which eventually allows you to invest in bigger/more profitable deals or to simply double down on your efforts and have two to three (or more) going at the same time. Side note: I once had 14 deals/rehabs in the works with 10 in the pipeline. Crazy few months that was! The key is to make sure you stay liquid, which you cannot do by plunking all of your capital into a buy-and-hold property. The buy-and-hold represents a commitment, or a deal you "marry" and preferably hold forever—for those of you who have been wondering when I was finally going to get around to explaining the meaning of this chapter's title.

Nothing wrong with getting married—I'm all for it—but not until you have that $1.2 million in cash that you need in order to reach your end goal. You also need to have the liquidity to be doing the incremental deals to build your savings quicker. You want to get "in and out" of deals fairly quickly, with a focus on growing your cash position—which means not getting tied down to a single property (getting married). If you're still working your 9-to-5, good for you: more gasoline to throw on the fire and you will reach your end goal quicker!

There is a saying that goes like this: "The best time to buy is now, and the best time to sell is never." Now that's a great saying and I use it frequently, but when you buy now and you hold, your cash is no longer liquid. You cannot use that money to go out and make more with it. (Similar to what I already explained with succumbing to the "American Dream" and buying a big house while at the same time getting into a ton of debt.) Only commit to that long-term relationship (buying and holding) when you're rich enough that you've got enough liquid capital left over to keep those short-term profit-generating deals going without a glitch.

And only get married to a particular property when you're sure you've truly found a keeper. That happens after you've done enough transactions that you can just tell there's something different about this one. It all just seems to feel right. The price, the amount of work, the street, the area, the cash flow, the potential for appreciation, the in-laws (you can even tell that your kids will be beautiful) … everything just falls perfectly into place. You will know it when that property comes along, and you will understand that is the property that you need to propose to and hold for eternity. Now, of course, you have to make sure that the property is going to get you a step closer to achieving your end goal, meaning it has to put money in your pocket every single month of every single year. It can't just look good, if you know what I mean. Wink, wink!

In my portfolio right now, I put a ring on one of those deals and got married. It looks like this: It's a 3-bedroom, 2-bath, 2-story brick beauty with 2,000 square feet and 1,700 square feet of unfinished attic space. It also comes situated on a double corner lot, has a double garage, a huge finished basement and it's a stone's throw away from the biggest and richest employer in town. I paid $30,000 (it needed zero work) for this property and it's currently tenanted for $1,200 per month to folks who have been there for four years now without a single hiccup. I got married to this property because it called out to me at night in a provocative French accent. (Joke!) I did it because as soon as I saw it, I knew that one day it had potential of becoming a 10-bed nursing home making me $100,000+ in yearly passive income on *just that one deal*. (I think I should change my name to David…)

Go for the High Cash Flow

The properties that you are going to buy and hold, the ones that will give you financial freedom status and serve you and your family for years, need to be high-cash-flowing properties. (Appreciation doesn't matter.) Ultimately, maybe 10 years down the road (maybe even sooner; it all depends on your efforts)—when you have done enough deals and accumulated enough liquid capital—it'll be time to park the majority of your money in buy-and-hold investment properties. And when you've finally reached that cash flow goal, you've achieved true financial freedom. Game over.

That is when you truly start living life on your terms. That is when you can do what you want, when you want, whenever you want, with who you want, and that is when you have succeeded. And that is *The Raw Truth*.

Now, let's get married and the real-life party can begin.

"The best time to buy real estate is NOW. The best time to sell is NEVER." (unless you prefer being single…)
— Unknown (With Engelo's twist)

Chapter 15

WHY MOST REALTORS SUCK

To be—or not to be—a real estate agent: That is a question that pops up on online forums and real estate investing sites all the time. In fact, I've written blogs myself on that very topic on my own website, on BiggerPockets.com and other platforms. While there are both pros and cons to a real estate investor having a real estate license, I come down squarely (and with a reverberating thud) on the side of *not* chaining myself to the constraints of regulatory overseers and brokers who can severely limit my ability to reach my end goal. (You always want to be in the driver's seat, navigated by your own GPS.)

How's that for a no-holds-barred introduction to the topic?

That said, though, I made my decision after carefully looking at the plusses and minuses. So, let's do the same now for your benefit.

Pros of Being a Licensed Real Estate Agent

First, let's look at the benefits of a real estate investor being licensed as a real estate agent:

- **Knowledge**—By virtue of the training classes you go through in order to become licensed, you end up with a lot of general knowledge not just about the ins and outs of real estate (working with buyers, sellers, lenders, title companies, etc.) but also the legalities. For example, you'll know how to properly write up contracts for buying and selling properties and you'll also learn the intricacies of Fair Housing laws.

- **Mentoring**—Hopefully, your broker will be someone who's got 20 or 30 years of experience and who is able—and willing—to guide you in your endeavors as a real estate agent. And in addition to the broker you work under, you also will have a network of real estate agents in the office of lots of other real estate professionals who are sharing processes and tips to help each other succeed in the business. (Your network equals your net worth.)

- **Access to the MLS**—This can be a real advantage, if you're an investor, because through the MLS you can easily pull reports on comps, view historic sales, market trends and other statistics to help you evaluate whether a property is going to be a good investment for you. (Although, as we discussed in Chapter 11, there *are* other ways you can get the information you need to evaluate a deal.) Most of the licensed real estate investors that I know tend to get their license just for the MLS access.

- **Commissions**—Ultimately, becoming a real estate agent is a sales job, and you can earn some amazing commissions, which will add more money to the table and enable you to reach your end goal quicker. There's nothing wrong with that, if it's truly something that you love doing. Not everybody does. Plus, you get to list your own properties for sale, which will save you some money in listing agent commissions.

Those are all good things. But you don't necessarily need a real estate license to succeed in the real estate business. Here are some of the possible negatives:

Cons of Being a Licensed Real Estate Agent

- It takes time and money to earn your license, and you generally must pass a state exam. (In some states it's easier and cheaper with various online options.)
- If you are a licensed agent working in a brokerage, you answer to your broker and will most likely be expected to do certain things and put in a certain amount of desk time. (You have to work under a broker for ages before you can actually become a broker yourself.)
- It can take quite some time before you get in the groove and start to make some sales and receive some commissions. (It can take years to build a good client base.)
- As a licensed agent, you must tell your broker about any property you buy off the MLS, and every brokerage has its own rules for their agents wanting to do so.
- When selling your own property you are required to disclose to all prospect buyers that you are a licensed real estate agent no matter where you market the listing (Craigslist, Facebook, etc. Buyers can take advantage of you, knowing that you are held to a higher standard and will have to negotiate/act by the book.)
- Your hours will primarily be set by clients' needs, which will include weekends.
- You are required to sit for a certain amount of Continuing Education hours each year.

- And finally, there is a lot more paperwork involved if you are a licensed agent. (You will have to shuffle paper till the cows come home.)
- So, in my view, the main reason that a real estate investor should *not* get a real estate license is that without one, you are truly working for yourself. You're free to conduct business in whatever way you want when it comes to buying and selling properties. You're not bogged down in paperwork and regulations. You don't have to meet the higher expectations and standards that real estate agents are held to.

Of course, even as a real estate investor you can't do anything illegal and you can't break any laws or regulations. You can make more money though, as a real estate investor by utilizing different investment strategies than you can by just being a real estate agent. Being a real estate investor does come with more risks because you are investing your own money. You have to put in time and money in order to make a profit. When you are a real estate agent, you don't have to invest your money, just your time to make a commission.

Now, it's perfectly OK with me if you prefer to be an agent and *not* an investor. Lots of people love being real estate agents solely—I have lots of them working in my own brokerage and they do really, really well. (Want to join my brokerage? Shameless plug #2.) I'm just saying that for investors, I don't see the advantage to having an agent's license in your back pocket.

Let Freedom Ring

I am a big believer in freedom. In freedom of speech, and in freedom of doing how you please. Of course, as long as you abide by the rules. Bend them, but don't ever break them.

Personally, I never really wanted to get my real estate license, because I don't believe that having a piece of paper and getting a certain degree or a certain license to operate is the ticket to success. I am big believer in having smarter people around me doing the things that I can't or don't want to do. In the real estate brokerage I am running right now, I leave the hands-on work to someone else whom I pay who is a licensed broker. (That person is an officer in the company of which I am the owner.)

Where there is a will, there's always a way. You don't necessarily need to have certain qualifications to succeed. If anything, sometimes those qualifications can limit what you can and cannot do.

I know that the title and theme of this chapter will make a lot of people mad and probably cost me a ton of business, but I just have to stress *The Raw Truth*. A lot of people perceive real estate agents to be as sleazy as secondhand-car salespeople. People are starting to hate them. Agents are not liked or respected as much as they were back in the day, and to be honest with you, I don't blame people for feeling that way. Here's why:

First of all, most real estate agents are lazy, in my opinion. They think the world owes them a favor, and they blame everything negative on their brokers. If they are not getting any leads or making any sales, it's the broker's fault. Now I ask you: Why in heaven's name would it be the broker's fault? Most brokers will teach you how to fish; why do you expect them to just hand you a fish? Go out there and catch your own fish! As in: Get your own leads! Another thing that won't hurt is replying to emails and calls promptly, honoring scheduled appointments and being on time. Too many agents are ignorant to the absolute basics of this "people business." (Head shake…)

I have said over and over again that real estate is a numbers game. In my opinion, being a successful real estate agent is easier than being a successful real estate investor. You just need to go out and knock on every single door in your area and give out your unique business cards. Just like politicians, you want to "shake hands and kiss babies" at every opportunity, and over time you will build familiarity in that local market. You will be on people's minds when they want to buy or sell a house. You will establish a local presence and you will also establish a book of business, and that book of business will lead to repeat business. Look different and talk different. Dress different. Be one-of-a-kind and make sure that you are remembered and always leave an impression that will lead to your success as a real estate agent.

Referrals Will Fuel Your Success

Once you start conducting good business and provide value to your clients by having their best interests at heart, that's when your business will grow through word of mouth and referrals. That is when you have hit the sweet spot. Unfortunately, not many agents are willing to put in the hard work to get the snowball effect of repeat business. Not many are willing to do the right thing by their clients, either.

The number one reason why most real estate agents suck, and why there is this stigma starting to surround being a real estate agent, is that so many of them don't really truly care about their sellers! Let's use a hypothetical example where a property is listed for $200,000. A listing agent gets a certain negotiated commission for that property ... let's say 6 percent. Now you, as the seller of the home, want to sell your property for as much as you possibly can. The real estate agent should be doing everything in their power to get you the best possible price. Unfortunately, that often isn't the case; most agents are prioritizing commissions and how many sales they make in a month much higher than your needs.

In an agent's eyes, and unfortunately, in that agent's pocket, there is not a significant difference in what they earn if your house sells for $190,000 instead of $200,000. On a $200,000 sale, the agent will make $12,000 if he or she is the listing and selling agent, meaning that agent found both the seller (you) and the buyer. If the house sells for

$190,000, the agent only makes $600 less. So that $10,000 doesn't make nearly as big a difference to the agent as it does to you. He or she might even be happy to take that $600 cut just to get the sale across the line and move on to the next client (victim).

Here's what you're going to starting hearing from them: "Oh, maybe we overpriced the property." Or, "It's a bit lower than you want, but I think you should accept this offer." Or maybe, "You know, we have been trying to get top dollar for a few months now, but we haven't been able to. So, you should seriously consider reducing your price." They don't care about you! All they care about is their commission, because $10,000 (or even more) off the asking price doesn't make a big difference to their bottom line, even though it makes a huge difference for you.

And that, my friends, pretty much summarizes why I think most real estate agents suck. All they are doing is chasing their commissions. They just want to move on to the next sucker ASAP. They don't really care about their clients or getting top-dollar for those clients. They are money-hungry, greedy jerks. Or at least 99% of them are, in my view. (The other 1% work in my brokerage, by the way. Just kidding!)

But I truly believe there's a light at the end of the tunnel. That is to say, these lazy agents are actually on the way to putting themselves out of business! Part of this is because of technological change that is happening in the industry every day. But more than that, it's the fact that consumers don't like having to pay agents for the privilege of selling their homes. We've already seen the beginning of this trend, as a number of startups are entering the niche and allowing people to list their properties for sale on their websites. The owners control who enters the houses by unlocking the lockbox via the internet. Who needs an agent? Not tech-savvy millennials and certainly not the many others who are disgruntled at the hassle of dealing with agents and having to pay large buyer's or seller's agent fees.

Now, having said that, I still believe that "people buy people," meaning personal interaction is key to selling a property, so this is still a ways off. But make no mistake: It's not a matter of "if," but rather of "when" this is going to happen.

What if You do Find a Good One?

Now in the meantime, when you do find a genuine real estate agent, that is someone with whom you should definitely conduct business for a very long time. And by all means, refer him or her to other people. Treat them like gold, because they are few and far between.

There aren't enough good ones in the business who are willing to compromise their commissions for the benefit of their clients. An agent should genuinely believe in the listing price, and if he or she thinks you're asking too much or will be a problematic client, that agent should never have taken on your listing or agreed to work with you in the first place. (For example: At any one of my companies the team is instructed to turn down more business than to take on. We can't help everyone. We don't see eye-to-eye with everyone and sometimes it's best for all parties to not work together.) Every agent should have their niche that they cater to, like overseas buyers or working with someone who's relocating for employment purposes, just to name a couple. Only work with individuals that you can genuinely offer assistance through your expertise.

In the end, be very careful and watch out for those who try to suck you in to get the listing and then drop you down on price. There are more of them out there than you might want to believe. And they're making a bad name for everybody else.

> *"Learn how to say NO to the good opportunities*
> *so you can say YES to the great ones."*
> — Engelo Rumora

Chapter 16

THE BIGGEST LIE IN REAL ESTATE

People who have met me know to not get me started on so-called real estate "gurus," the sleazebags who profit from taking your money to teach you real estate "secrets." I tell you what, I am the biggest anti-guru known to mankind! (Just in case you haven't noticed with all of my guru rants from the previous chapters…)

In my mind, the biggest, most disgusting fraud, scam, lie, piece of trash out there is anyone who's trying to sell you on courses, seminars, DVDs, even books with a hidden agenda on how to "get rich" in real estate. I mean, the list of B.S. guru wizardry materials can go on forever. One huge scam that has been going on for a very long time now is these supposed gurus on reality-TV flipping shows—the majority of them, anyway.

Credibility is Born in the Trenches

We see them on television, and then all of a sudden that gives them instant credibility? Give me a freaking break! Wake up, people! I have a real problem with that since I am in the trenches every day, actually doing real estate investing rather than just playing in character as an investor on TV. And my firsthand experiences are far different from what is portrayed on-screen. Believe me when I say that almost everything about those shows is misrepresented, if not outright fake. That's *The Raw Truth*. If you don't believe me (which you should by now), ask any experienced real estate investor and see what they say.

So, maybe you watch one of those fix-and-flip reality shows and then you see an ad somewhere (social media, most likely) inviting you to a free 2-hour seminar on how to "Flip to Riches." You sign yourself and your spouse up because you see yourselves renovating houses, wearing expensive watches and getting manicures and making $50,000 to $100,000 profit on each house (even though those numbers are hardly as commonplace as the TV shows claim).

I Challenge You to Find a Legitimate Guru

Do me a favor and Google every guru's name you come across and put the word "scam" behind it. If you find even one legitimate "guru" out there, please let me know, as I have yet to find anyone who has a clean background. I would love to personally meet the true exception. (Make sure to check the first three pages of the Google search.)

Here's how it typically works, according to the Better Business Bureau, which logs way too many consumer complaints every year about unfulfilled promises from real estate gurus:

So, you take this free 2-hour seminar and the next thing they try to sell you on is a one-day event, for which you have to pay around $1,500. At that event, they give you a little more content, but nothing that you couldn't find out for yourself by reading a genuine book, contributing to a real estate forum or doing research online. Then from that one-day $1,500 event, you get up-sold to a 3-day mastermind retreat, where "all secrets" will supposedly be revealed.

At the 3-day mastermind, you get a ton of stuff thrown in your face, from investment properties to LLC setups to self-directed IRA accounts, "How-to's" on increasing your credit card limit to whatever other jargon they can find just to make a dime. Let's not even go into the charge of between $25,000 and $50,000 (looks like that credit card limit came in handy, right?) to attend the 3-day retreat where you will supposedly learn everything and anything about flipping. Wrong, wrong, wrong!

And a funny thing about it is, the celebrities that you all love and look up to from the TV shows usually don't even show up. They might show up via some lame Skype interview or pre-recorded video message, but sometimes they don't even do that. This is the biggest scam in real estate, and it has been running for a very long time, and there is no end in sight because there are always going to be suckers out there buying into these lies. I surely hope that doesn't include you.

Check out this "Golden Nugget." Step back and think about it this way: Why the hell is someone selling me a course on how to do it if they can just go out and do it themselves and make 10 times more that way than they can from selling the course? Hello...

Let me repeat that. Why is someone selling me a course, for let's say $5,000, on "how to flip a house" if they can actually go out and do it themselves and make 10 times more?

Those Who Can't Do, 'Teach'

Here's your answer: They can't do it, because it's a scam. It's a lie. It's fluff. These sleazebags make more money selling you a how-to course than actually doing it themselves. It's a cycle.

These "celebrities" sell their souls for a fortune to marketing companies and seminar companies, and they don't control the process at all or any of the teachings (not that they would be any good even if they did). Other professional salespeople take over, and they use hardcore pressure tactics to sell you in the most disgusting way possible at all of these events. They will force you to max out your credit cards paying for all their useless "necessities." I have heard stories of people committing suicide afterward for losing all that money. Terrible!

Here is what I believe in: If you're sick, you go to the doctor. The doctor gets you better. If your car breaks down, you take it to a mechanic, who fixes it. You don't buy a course on how to fix your car, and you definitely don't attend a seminar on how to get yourself better from the flu.

If you want to learn how to make money in real estate, first of all, look in your local area and identify the biggest players in town. Then go and beg them to let you clean their shoes and wash their cars so you can brush shoulders with them every day and learn what they do and how they do it.

Or if you are going to spend any kind of money, spend the money with someone who is actually making money doing deals, *every day*. They might be willing to coach or consult you one-on-one. You can call them. You can email them. You can meet them in person. (Shameless plug #3: I do consulting and it's ridiculously expensive. It's to turn people away so that I can actually stay busy doing deals. But if you really insist…)

That is the only kind of money that I see you spending on any kind of "real estate guru." Everything else is garbage.

"Price is what you pay, value is what you get."
— Warren Buffett

Chapter 17

YOUR ATTORNEY AND ACCOUNTANT ARE THIEVES

Have you ever heard the saying that attorneys (or accountants) have a license to steal? Well, guess what? It's because they do. Or at least it seems like that to me every time I look at an invoice from one of them.

When I started my journey as a real estate investor, my mentors told me to not overcomplicate things in the beginning. Ultimately, you have nothing to lose when you first start, and you probably are not going to have much to lose for a while. Don't spend money or energy getting into complex legal or accounting and bookkeeping relationships at first.

You need to put all of your focus and resources into doing deals, driving revenue and sales, and making profits, because those profits—and that money in your account—will allow you to do numerous things. It will allow you to focus on buying multiple properties, doing more deals at the same time, increasing your marketing efforts, by spending money on lead generation and maybe even hiring a few people.

So, don't get fancy. Find yourself a little mini-office or shared workspace. Hire an admin person (but only if you can comfortably afford one) who can help you with some basic paperwork and scheduling or whatever else it may be. I can't stress enough how important it is to keep costs at an absolute minimum. Even to this day, my staff is instructed to dispute unknown $2 credit card charges. (It's $2 today but could be $2,000 tomorrow.) Doing the small things well and consistently will enable the big things to fall into place. Attention to detail, mates. Anyway, I think you get my drift here. Moving on …

Ultimately, in my opinion, you do not need to clutter yourself with complex legal and accounting strategies until you've actually got a legitimate real estate business operation up and running. Lawyers and accountants can nickel-and-dime you to death, and there's really no way to protect yourself against their fees when that's how they charge and all they have to "sell" is their time.

Take Steps to Protect Yourself

Here are a couple of simple tips that you can use to protect yourself from getting gouged:

- If you need a certain legal task accomplished (for example, doing an eviction or reviewing a contract), agree in advance about how much it's going to cost. This is a strategy that we use when we want an upfront breakdown of how much time something is going to take and what the hourly rate is going to be.

- Never—and I mean never with a capital N—go into working with any accountant or attorney with an open checkbook. (This means a signed contract for a monthly retainer.) Every email you send, every text message, every phone call, they track how long it takes them to read, respond and execute. You'll get fees in increments of .10 of an hour, and you'll be dropping $30, $40, $50 for every little text message or email you send. That can add up to monthly bills of $2,000 or $3,000 or $5,000+. Just don't do it. (Not too long ago we had a "high-end" accounting firm get us for $9,000. They spent $5,000 of that "preparing to prepare to prepare" for a meeting. No kidding.)

You should only start getting involved in things like complex accounting strategies and business structures (S Corp and C Corp mumbo jumbo) and trust accounts and protecting your assets and who knows what else once you've actually got something to lose. And whatever that "something" is, you are the one who has to decide when you need to start spending big dollars to protect it. My advice would be that it's fine to get very serious with legal and accounting matters once you have made your first $1 million in revenue. Then you have a budget that can actually afford it. But until then, DIY as much as you can. Or ask for free pointers from other investors like me who spend thousands every month on lawyers and accountants. (Ultimately, if you live in fear that you're going to get sued, well, I honestly think that is going to prevent you from taking risks and doing deals and making money.) Just always do the right thing and you should be fine. If you make a mistake, own up to it and pay for it. People can be very forgiving as long as you "admit and fix." Man, oh man, have I made some mistakes and thank God to this day I have never been sued.

You should be the gas in this business you're driving, not the brakes. Get someone else on your team to be the brakes, to be the devil's advocate. (Your spouse would be perfect!) That person doesn't necessarily have to be an attorney. In the meantime, run your business in a legitimate way. Be ethical. Don't do anything stupid. When you're wrong, apologize and pay for your mistakes. Don't ask for permission, though, before you want to do something because it never gets granted; beg for forgiveness when you are in the wrong.

Now, don't get me wrong. I'm not saying you shouldn't speak with an accountant or an attorney. By all means, consult with them. What I am saying is, don't go and overcomplicate things and take your eye off the prize. Don't forget your end goal. Don't forget your cash flow figure. Focus on those things first and foremost. Over the years I have witnessed too many investors never getting over the "legal hurdle." Just walk around it for now and you can always come back to jump it later. It's better to try and fail than to never try something at all. Then, when you finally get to the stage where you believe you have something to lose or a monthly budget that can be allocated to other things, you can start dumping money into complex legal and accounting strategies as long as they too will progress you in a faster yet safer way to achieving your end goal.

A great rule of thumb is this: Always focus on the working money. Don't focus on idle money, and paying your accountant and attorney is all idle money. Yes, it can save you a lot in the long run, but I'll tell you right now, unless you buy a property, fix it, sell it and make a profit, you can't afford your accountant and attorney in the first place and you have "nothing to save." So, you might as well not even think about it until you can actually afford to pay their exorbitant fees. Learn how to do real estate first. Then you can put your "legal pants" on.

I Prefer to Play Offense

I am not a defensive-type real estate investor; I am an offensive-type real estate investor. So, my opinion is that you are better off spending money on something that can actually give you a return for that investment immediately. Investing $10,000, $15,000, $20,000 in legal and accounting advice ultimately is for the purpose of saving you money in the long run. But what money in the long run are you going to save if you're not actually making money? So that $10,000, $15,000 or $20,000 is better spent on something that can make you $10,000, $15,000 or $20,000. That could be new marketing strategies (website, videos, branding), booths, speaking engagements. That could be lead-generation strategies (yellow-letter campaigns, Google and Facebook ads). That could be buying and fixing another property, or whatever it is. Figure it out, Bob and Mary! Ultimately, I want you to focus on the "today" money and *what makes you money right now* and not the idle money.

Once you do decide that it's time to really put on your legal and accounting pants, you need to find an accountant or attorney who is honest, aggressive, experienced and knowledgeable about what you do. One tip? Seek out one who has real estate investing experience. Otherwise, you're going to be wasting each other's time. It took me five tries (both attorney and accountant) to get to the ones that I have today. A very important thing to me is speed. So, if they take too long with a certain task or objective, I am forced to move on. That usually suggests that they are too busy and can't handle the demand. And as I initially said, you want professionals who will give you rates in advance. If there is any way you can avoid those .1-hour charges, that would be great.

Another thing to consider is this: How can you get your accountant or attorney vested in your success? For example, I've given equity in one of my businesses to one of my attorneys, and in return he discounted his hourly rate. Not just that, I've sucked him into my business now. So, he's not going to check his watch as often. (I actually told him to throw out his watch. True story.) Another arrangement that we have with our accountant is a "sliding scale" payment plan. The more revenue our companies generate, the more he gets paid. This is great because he is super-proactive and always suggesting additional income-generating strategies. So, he is working more so as a CFO (chief financial officer).

Stay on Top of Things!

In terms of accounting, beware of the many bookkeeping companies that will charge a flat monthly fee to do your books and get their in-house accountant to file your taxes. This proved to be a disastrous move for us. The books were nonstop wrong. We spent more time answering their questions than they probably spent actually doing the work. And they had no real estate experience whatsoever. Plus, nothing was ever up-to-date and we "flew blind" for ages. There is nothing worse than not knowing where you stand from a financial standpoint. Disaster! Whatever route you choose, make sure you keep up with it. A good idea would be to get every bit of work/advice confirmed by two or three other attorneys or accountants. Yes, it will cost more, but this way you will know if your accountant, bookkeeper or attorney is doing a good job. What you don't want to happen is for your books or legals to be wrong, because if that happens, you're going to be charged an absolute fortune by someone else to go back and fix it all.

I'm telling you this from firsthand experience. You don't want to go there. It's an absolute nightmare! That's *The Raw Truth*.

With that said, I screwed up my legals and accounting for years and had to pay a fortune in fees to backtrack and fix it all. Would I have gone about it any differently knowing now what I didn't know back then? No way. Because doing it "correctly" from the start and spending, let's say, $20,000 on legal/accounting fees would have wiped me out. That $20,000 helped me get to where I am today (money makes money).

Paying $50,000 nowadays just to fix stuff really sucks. But we were able to do it without affecting our bottom line too much.

Now you know why I believe that your accountant and attorney are thieves. You know what? Even your bookkeeper. Let's throw that into the mix...

> *"If curiosity kills the cat,*
> *procrastination kills an investor's dream."*
> — Engelo Rumora

Chapter 18

DON'T SCREW WITH UNCLE SAM

Some of the weirdest stuff I have ever heard of is something that has been going on in Australia's real estate market for a while. It's called "negative gearing," where investors will invest in properties to lose money intentionally.

Yeah, you read that correctly: They are losing money on purpose. I can hardly believe it, too. I mean, I just want to grab them by the shoulders and shake them like a rag doll, screaming, "What the hell are you doing?!"

The thinking is that if you invest in a property where the monthly expenses are going to be more than the income is, then whatever you lose every year on that particular property gets offset against your personal income. You can offset the taxes that you have to pay with how much money you've lost through that negatively geared property. And those investors hope that the property itself—while it is losing them money every month—is also going to appreciate in value more than the amount they actually lose.

Whoever invented this cockamamie theory, I don't know, but it is the weirdest, stupidest stuff I have ever heard of in my whole life.

Don't Play This Fool's Game!

Sorry to disappoint you, mates, but this chapter isn't about "how to minimize your taxes." For that you should buy a book written by an accountant (who wrote it from his/her jail cell. Just saying…). If you are using that negative-gearing strategy merely to save money on taxes, that's just nuts. There is something wrong here. Who in their right mind would want to be incurring losses on their investments just to save on taxes? Why would you select a property based on a "depreciation schedule?" That is absolutely mind-boggling to me.

We should invest in real estate to make money. We should invest in real estate to make the most amount of money we possibly can on every single deal we do and which is in our portfolio.

And as I have tried to make abundantly clear, I firmly believe the way to do that is through first, saving $50,000 to $100,000, and then using that cash—not leverage—to purchase a property at substantially below-market value (20–30 cents on the dollar), rehab it and sell for a tidy profit. Rinse and repeat.

And remember: You've got to do your research; know your market inside and out so you can recognize the right property in the right area, for the right price, needing the right amount of rehab work. I base my figures on the live pulse that I feel from my local market on a daily basis and so should you.

I don't care about depreciation. I invest in real estate to make as much money as I possibly can. I want to buy as many properties as I possibly can and make as much profit as possible on every deal. I don't care at all about saving money on taxes. Real estate investing in general already is a great way to minimize your taxes, and I'm proud to pay Uncle Sam his fair share. In fact, the more the better. And that's *The Raw Truth.*

The Bigger My Tax Bill, the Better

I hear so many people always complaining about taxes. Do you know that the U.S. has some of the lowest taxes of any country? Look it up.

I hope that I have to pay $10 million in taxes one day, because that will probably mean that I am making $100 million in profits. The rich don't pay much in taxes; it's true and we all know it. It's just the elephant in the room that nobody ever points out.

The more money you make, the less you pay in taxes. Yes, "less!"

So I want to pay an absolute fortune in taxes because that will mean I'm doing something right and that I'm making an absolute fortune also. (It sounds weird but it's true.)

But for you to invest in something that's losing money, while you *hope* that the value appreciates? I still don't understand it. As I have said previously, hope is not a strategy!

Now, for everyone on the East Coast and West Coast of the United States, your markets have boomed in the years since the housing crisis. They've gone up in value a massive amount. Still, it is mind-boggling to me that you are now investing in these expensive properties at all, most likely losing money on your monthly mortgage repayments, which means your income is not covering your expenses. But you are doing that because of some prediction and hope that the property is going to appreciate in value more than you are losing on your mortgage repayments. The market has already recovered, mates. Remember the mantra, "Buy low, sell high." Wake up. Please stop thinking that you are Nostradamus. You can't predict the future.

Investing in such a way is not smart or strategic. It's purely speculative. The casino is always open if you like to gamble, so be my guest and bet on black for me. Because that's where I'll always be. (In the black.)

There's No Such Thing as Luck

And regarding that thing that so many investors rely on, called "luck"—I don't believe in it. As I see it, investors should make their own luck by hustling every day and not waiting for the market to appreciate. "He or she got lucky" is a poor-person mentality that judges other successful people. Leave the "getting lucky" to those folks for when they play the lottery. You, on the other hand, "rise and grind." I love the quote by Ray Kroc: "I sure was an 'overnight' success. But 30 years is a long night."

Remember, we invest in real estate to supplement the income we are getting from a job we do not want to be working in. So why are you investing for capital appreciation? That will not supplement your income. That is intangible. It is equity; today it's there, and tomorrow it could be gone. Don't allow the economy to dictate your destiny.

How many times have I said it already? We don't know where the market is going. We can't predict the future.

Invest on Today's Numbers

The numbers in the deal as they stand today, however, are always true. That's why the smartest thing you can do is invest based on today's numbers and the numbers of that particular transaction. Your income has to outweigh your expenses (the more it outweighs them, the better). There has to be positive cash flow left over (if you're using leverage), and there has to be a ton of money pouring into your pocket every single month. And I mean a ton.

Before investing and when crunching the numbers on a deal, be sure to ask yourself questions like, "What is my purchase price of that particular property?" and "What are my expenses?" Always include a margin of safety, meaning underestimate your income and overestimate your expenses. If the bottom line meets your end goal—if you buy the property and add to your portfolio—is it getting you a step closer to where you need to be, cash flow-wise? We live off cash flow, not capital appreciation and equity. Never forget that. Become obsessed with repetitively self-questioning. It will help with making sure that you are on the right path—the path that you initially chose but might have been sidetracked from.

Invest based on cash flow; invest based on making an absolute fortune! And when you make more money, pay your taxes fair and square. I said that the tax system favors business owners and folks doing well, so I'm sure you'll have other tax advantages you can use through a good accountant.

Don't be scared to pay Uncle Sam. Pay him. Expense what you legally can expense. Be smart about your accounting, but pay your taxes fairly. Paying them quarterly is really smart; do it in advance if you need to. Uncle Sam will be happy and proud.

You don't want to get audited, because that's an absolute nightmare. It's just like if a cop follows you around long enough, eventually that officer will catch you doing something illegal and you'll get in trouble. Being audited is the same. We all make mistakes; make sure yours are honest ones, though, and that will get you out of major trouble.

Be proud to be American because there are so many others who would die to be in your shoes.

"God bless America. It's the best country in the world.
Try making a living or just living in another country
and I'll see you back here shortly..."
— Engelo Rumora

Chapter 19

APPRAISERS AND BUILDING INSPECTORS ARE B.S. ARTISTS

Now, before I launch into this next rant (the last one of the book, I promise), I will acknowledge that there may in fact be a purpose and a place for appraisers and building inspectors. It's just not in any place where I do business and hope to make any money.

It really sucks that when some folks are given a bit of authority, they tend to consider themselves to be rulers of the world. Such people are a joke, in my eyes. Respect is earned over time and by doing the right thing. Your ego should never blossom because of a title you hold. You can let it blossom once you prove yourself with results. Even then, stay humble and tame the ego. It will keep jealous people away.

By far, appraisers and building inspectors have been the biggest source of frustration (and that's putting it mildly!) to me in my journey as a real estate investor. (And I'm sure to many other experienced investors.)

My goal—and it should be yours, too, as a real estate investor—is to make money. To find profitable deals and do them quickly so I can move on to the next, and the next, and the next so that I reach my end goal in the shortest amount of time.

But sadly, appraisers and building inspectors have instead represented huge roadblocks—to me, anyway. It's as if they take their greatest satisfaction in finding problems where there are none, which ends up costing me massive amounts of both time and money. They are like pigeons. They "fly in" to the property, do a few "drops" and then they fly away, leaving a huge mess in their shadow along with bringing all my business momentum to a grinding halt. And for what?

Now, theoretically, these professionals are supposed to make the system run more smoothly and keep everybody on a level playing field. Appraisers are supposed to provide a realistic picture of what a property is worth so nobody on either end gets cheated. And you expect building inspectors to identify areas of structural concern that truly should be corrected so no one gets hurt—physically or financially.

Where Did Good Intentions Go Awry?

But somewhere along the line, those good intentions got really, truly, undeniably screwed up. My theory is that you can trace it back to the housing downturn that precipitated the Great Recession and the entire global financial crisis. Yes, I agree, it would be too simplistic to blame it *all* on appraisers. But nevertheless, I truly believe they were major contributors (I don't even want to talk about the idiot lenders, as that's a book on its own) to the problems that came from that meltdown.

I don't want to get mired in an in-depth history lesson here, but suffice it to say that prior to and during the housing crash there was a lot of shenanigans and CYA going on. A lot of appraisers were right in the middle of that, taking bribes from mortgage brokers and lenders to inflate values and put in their own numbers and heaven knows what else. That's why a lot of them went to jail for fraud.

And as fallout from that, some appraisers today are so worried about job security that they go in the opposite direction with their numbers (they tend to be ridiculously conservative). Because they don't want to be investigated if they appraise a property that later goes into foreclosure, they are being absolutely unrealistic with their valuations of particular properties. To cover their butts they may even go to the extent of using the prices received from foreclosures, which are distressed and unrenovated properties in a particular area, as comparables to the property they are appraising.

It is common practice these days, in my experience, for an appraiser to undervalue a property by $10,000 or more (depending on the median house price in your market; the $10,000 mentioned is for the Ohio market), costing the buyer and seller time, money, and worst of all, unnecessary heartache.

Unfortunately, there is nothing we can do about this, because lenders get to choose the appraisers at their own discretion. They no longer allow you, the borrower, to make the appraiser selection like they did back in the day. So, you are stuck if the appraisal comes back putting you over a giant barrel.

I see nothing wrong with selling a property for a price that someone is willing and able to pay/afford. Do you?

To make things worse, the "12-month rule" of Fannie Mae complicates things further. This is the general guideline that says the sales of properties used as comparables should ideally be dated within 12 months of the current transaction date. While exceptions are allowed, the fact of the matter is that it is much easier to fall back on this rule and avoid having to put in the extra paperwork or other heavy lifting. (Appraisers, you are totally lazy! Some of you.)

Let me give you an example. Let's say we are appraising House A, a renovated (to perfection) 3-bedroom, 1-bathroom home, 1,200 square feet, in an area heavily hit with foreclosures (and there are a lot of areas in the country like that even now). The selling price of House A is $100,000. That's the information the appraiser has to start with.

Let's say that within the previous 12 months, there were three similar properties in the area (all within a 1-mile radius) that have been foreclosed on and were distressed (absolute losers). Let's call them Houses B, C and D. Like House A, they are 3-bedroom, 1-bath homes, about 1,200 square feet. They each sold at foreclosure for $30,000. Does that mean the value of House A should be determined by this price ($30,000)?

Let's say there also were three additional properties, call them Houses E, F and G. They also are 3-bedroom, 1-bath, 1,200-square-foot homes in the same neighborhood. These are closer to House A and within a half-mile radius. They were sold 15, 17 and 19 months ago. They are all renovated comparables, similar to House A (maybe not as nice), and they sold for $60,000, $80,000 and $90,000. Which houses are truly the more comparable?

What is very sad is that so many appraisers choose the easy way out and dismiss these more-relevant properties because the sales are more than 12 months old. The appraiser instead uses the three foreclosed and distressed homes that sold within the last 12 months. This can severely affect the value of House A. Not just that, but as time goes on, don't prices tend to go up in value? They usually do, so a basic assumption should be that House A is worth even more now since enough time has passed than when the older comparables (Houses E, F, and G) sold.

Where's the Sense in That?

There's just no common sense to this method, especially if we start mentioning all the deductions and additions they can use. For example: If House A has a "new" AC unit, "finished" basement and "converted" attic, that would automatically increase the property's value substantially. Of course that could be true, but can you see how many of those items are easily manipulated? They can twist things in any way they feel fit, and use whatever comparable sales or deductions they want. Some will even go as far as—and intentionally, out of jealousy—to appraise for less. Just because they know that an investor bought House A for a great price and "couldn't possibly deserve to make that much in profit." Don't forget that they have access to all of the information: How much you bought it for and how much you spent on the rehab. Yep, it's happened to me before, many times. They wanted to limit my profit with their low appraisal. What the hell, right?

In my mind, appraisers are absolute freaking B.S. artists (the Warhols) … unbelievable!

And that brings me to an even bigger bunch of B.S. artists: The building inspectors (the Picassos).

Building inspectors are paid to find faults. Have you ever, *ever*, *ever* received a building inspection without a fault listed on it? I'll bet you anything that your answer is no, and you never will, because it won't happen. It doesn't matter whether you renovated that property perfectly, or whether you got the best builder to build it from the ground up with all-new eco-friendly "titanium, gold, diamond" materials. There will still be faults. Even if that fault just consists of a quarter-sized hole in the siding, for instance, I know of inspectors who will take a close-up photo of it, frame a red box around the photo with an arrow, and in the fine print (red-color, bold-font, write a note that says "consult a structural engineer to thoroughly inspect," thereby protecting their own behinds. Yep, because you never know what outer space vacuum of dark matter could suck the galaxy through that tiny black hole, creating another Big Bang.

They'll do this exercise over and over again, just to justify the price paid for conducting a building inspection, even though that minor fault has nothing to do with the sustainability of that property. Building codes that inspectors go to change at a rapid pace, so sometimes the faults found in an inspection—which would scare any normal human being reading it—are not required to be rectified as per the current "new" building codes. In my opinion, most of these folks just don't really care and are too lazy to keep up with the ever-changing code. It's just too easy "slapping" a few photos and some B.S. in a report and charging $500 for it. Sometimes I feel they should get paid even more for the creativity. I mean, it takes time coming up with so much fantasy.

Warren Buffett says that "the weakest link in a chain" is the one that causes a problem, meaning that when one link is faulty, the entire chain is useless and breaks. In this instance, if you want to sell a property to someone who needs to get a mortgage, which requires that the property have an appraisal and a building inspection done, you are opting for a strategy that has multiple links in its chain. If one of those links is faulty—i.e., the appraisal doesn't come in, the building inspection isn't acceptable, the lender drags their feet, the buyer screws up and doesn't get approved for the loan—your chain can be useless, and you may never get that transaction done; the deal could break. Or in the best-case scenario, significant delays will occur, with higher selling costs to you.

Identify and Eliminate the Weak Links

Something I have believed very strongly from the day I started my journey in real estate is that if you can't beat something, you have to eliminate it. So, the big question here is, how do you eliminate this ugly situation?

That's a tough one, and no one answer "fits all." Especially when it comes to the various real estate strategies out there, with most of them being dependent on the "sham show" that we get from building inspectors and appraisers.

Here is my solution and something that I do, so take it for what it is: You sell on your terms. You sell properties to investors. This could mean selling renovated properties to buy-and-hold investors or wholesaling properties to buy-fix-and-flip investors. They'll often buy for all cash, and they'll buy without any contingencies (or you request that they do). When they don't have to go through a loan approval process, there's no need for inspection and appraisal, no worry that the paperwork will hold things up or that one tiny fault could "break" your entire transaction. Plus, investors tend to be much more knowledgeable on property buying than the average mom and pop homebuyer. Their tolerance to risk is higher and they just "get it."

You have to be the best in order to set such terms. When I first started my company, it took me a year and a half to make my first sale. Even back then, I stayed true to my beliefs and never compromised. My terms were "my terms," and it was a "take it or leave it" approach. Eventually we sold a property, and another, and another. We made those investors raving fans of our business, and before you know it, the word spread like wildfire and we snowballed. Be the best and you will get to work with the best. Oh, and be very transparent in your dealings. Since no appraisal or inspection is being done, it's up to you to show that the property is renovated to a great standard and that you are selling it for fair market value. You should go above and beyond what an appraiser or inspector would to provide all of those findings to your investor-buyer.

I have to say, I much prefer playing by my rules and according to my timetable. It makes the game of real estate investing a whole lot more fun, efficient and profitable for everyone involved.

When it comes to outside influences, we real estate investors must limit ourselves as much as we possibly can. The more links you add to your chain, the higher the probability of something going wrong and it breaking.

Control as much as you can of the entire process and do the right thing by everyone you work with and then you will truly be an artist in your craft. And that's *The Raw Truth.*

"If you build it, he will come."
— From the movie *Field of Dreams*, starring Kevin Costner

Chapter 20

BEWARE OF THE DEVIL IN DISGUISE

I hope you don't mind dancing with devil, because you'll probably have to if you truly want to advance your real estate endeavors to new heights.

Jokes aside, how many of you out there really, truly want to be dealing with tenants and toilets? Getting phone calls at all hours of the night or on weekends from someone renting one of your investment properties, whining about how a lightbulb just burned out, or a neighbor's tree fell on their dog, or some other lame matter?

Of course I'm offering up outrageous scenarios only to make a point (once you've been in real estate long enough, you will hear and see it all), because we all know that there *are* times when a tenant has a maintenance emergency that *does* need genuine attention.

But the point is, do you really want to be the person who gets that call? ("That dreaded call" that kills your heart and soul right there and then and completely disrupts your schedule, peace and your life.)

I'll bet the answer is no, you don't want to be bothered with anything except watching the cashflow from your properties just roll in like dice at a casino on a hot streak.

And that, my mates, is why you, Mr. or Ms. Real Estate Investor, need a property management company—the "Devil" that is always stuck in the middle between tenants (the "bad" people) and landlords (the "good" people). A property management company will take care of the maintenance issues and also the day-to-day operational needs associated with your property, such as screening prospective tenants, running background checks, setting up the various accounts, collecting rent, even evicting deadbeats if need be—along with a whole list of other crap that, trust me when I say this, you just don't want to be doing. Think of property management companies as the necessarily evil.

There. Now that I've established that property management is essential to success in buy-and-hold real estate investing, I have something else very important to add:

Property management companies will gladly screw you if you let them. And that's just *The Raw Truth*.

Unfortunate Truths About Property Management Companies

I can tell you from my battle-scarred firsthand experience:

Property management companies are known to nickel-and-dime investors to death.

They will make up non-existent repairs just to charge stupid fees.

They are notorious for up-charging way more than they should, even if there isn't any legitimate reason to do so.

They'll charge you a management fee even when the property is vacant.

They're known for hiring unethical, thieving employees who'll steal rent payments and then just freaking disappear. And then, of course, the property management company will not take responsibility.

Most aren't licensed to manage and do not abide by the state's Division of Real Estate rules.

Many will compromise the various accounts required to run a transparent operation.

Some just empty all the company's bank accounts and disappear (yep, it happens quite often, believe it or not).

The list goes on, but I think you get the point.

I'd say 99 percent of property management companies are totally shady. They do not correspond in a transparent or timely manner with their clients—the landlords. They do not respond to tenants' requests in a timely manner, either. And even those that do are so sloppy and negligent about it that the properties start to look like they are run by slumlords.

How do I know? Because all of that has happened to me in my own real estate investing journey.

When I was still in Australia, I started out investing here in the U.S. by buying a few turnkey properties in Rochester, N.Y., and in Kansas City. The turnkey providers from whom I bought those investment properties said they handled all the property management responsibilities, but what they didn't say was that they contracted those services out to third-party property managers rather than handling everything in-house.

Third-Party Property Managers Don't Care About You

The problem there is that when buying turnkey, third-party property management companies (or most property management companies in general) do not really have a genuine interest in making sure the property is performing as promised by the turnkey provider or that they are minimizing all of the expenses they possibly can to benefit the property owner—the investor. They simply do not have a vested interest in your long-term success. They just don't care.

Why not? Because they're in it to make money—as much of it as they can, and they do that by charging fee upon fee for every little thing you can imagine: monthly management, lease renewals, tenant placement, maintenance, other administrative costs, and on and on.

Some get so super-creative that you don't even know what/how they are charging you.

It's black magic, I'm telling you!

Now, this isn't just risky for the investor, it can be disastrous for the partnering turnkey investment company as well. There are many horror stories on that front also. A quick Google search will reveal them to you.

Over the years, I've witnessed countless turnkey companies lose their reputation because of the shady dealings of their third-party property management vendors, because they've got no control over what the property manager does. When the turnkey company doesn't own the property management arm of their business, then they don't fully control their own fate, their own destiny. That property management company can send that turnkey company—and your investment with it—right down the drain by lifting their fees whenever they want and for whatever they want, and there's nothing you or the turnkey provider can do about it.

Why Not Just Do-It-Yourself?

Now, some of you may be thinking, "Well, the way to avoid all that is to simply do it myself."

NO, NO, NO, NO!!!!

WRONG!!!!!

Do you really think you can self-manage? Do you really think you can do all of the things I've just mentioned—screening tenants, collecting rent, doing maintenance, balancing the books, etc.—better than a group of people who specialize in doing that all day, every day? And for what? To save a few pennies?

Have you ever heard the saying "What is your time worth?"

My question to all you DIYers is this: What the hell are you focusing on?

Are you focusing on dealing with tenants and toilets? Are you focusing on collecting rents? Calling maintenance guys to do the repairs? Listening to tenant complaints at freaking midnight? Is that your focus?

Is that why you got into this game?

Is that you want to be doing long-term?

Forever?

Let's review what this entire book has been about: Your focus should be on growing your portfolio. On chasing that end goal. On finding deals. On establishing relationships with key people. On adding more properties to your book of business. On growing your cashflow just like the muscles of a body builder on steroids.

In short, on real estate investing!

If you want passive income, get the right people to do the work for you so you can be where you want, when you want, doing what you want—all the while letting that passive income steam into your bank account every month like a freight train (I'm on a roll in this chapter with my analogies. I hope you don't mind...).

"Now wait just a darn minute, Engelo," you might be saying. "You've just spent most of this chapter telling me how crooked and unethical property management companies are, and yet you're advising me to turn my investment operations over to them? What the hell?"

Yes, exactly!

My point, mates, is that you have to find the *right* property management company—the "Angel" property management company that will bless your portfolio for eternity. If you're investing through a turnkey company, make sure that it is a *true* turnkey company, meaning one whose property management operation is in-house and solely owned or controlled by the turnkey provider. And not through some shady third-party property manager.

If you're doing investments on your own, then find a reputable property management company to whom you can outsource those responsibilities.

Let's face it: it's not that hard for anyone to find, buy, fix and sell a house. After a bit of time spent playing the game, pretty much anyone can do it. The hardest part in real estate—and the most important thing to an investor's ongoing success—is good property management for the long term. Not finding the deal, buying it, nor renovating the property well, but actually being able to place tenants who are going to stay and pay, being able to quickly meet those tenants' demands, fix whatever needs to be fixed, collect the rents, distribute the rents correctly and just manage the property well for the long haul.

Property management can be a very thankless job at times, and to be honest, I understand why so many turn to the "dark side." There is just not enough money in it unless you cheat and nickel-and-dime. Plus, pretty much everyone from tenants to landlords is hating on you, and it's super-hard keeping the morale of employees high when every phone call is a bashing, be it from a disgruntled tenant or a disgruntled landlord.

It's a true blessing finding that angel company that does a decent job and allows you to live a worry-free life.

Your valuable time is far better spent on scaling your portfolio—on finding more and better deals, because the more properties that you have in a portfolio, the less you will feel the impact of the many miscellaneous fees that a property management company charges, and the less you will feel the impact of a property when it goes vacant or when any repairs need to be done.

Don't trip over dollars to pick up pennies. Even the angel company won't be perfect and will make mistakes. Sometimes probably even charging for things that they shouldn't.

Just consider this the cost of doing business.

It should be your number one priority to build your portfolio as big as you can, as quickly as you can. But you should definitely not think that you are saving money by self-managing, because you're not, and that's why property management is the Devil in Disguise.

How Do You Find an Angel?

So here's the key question I want to answer for you: How can you identify a *good, ethical* property management company, anyway?

Whether this is a division of your turnkey provider or is a stand-alone property management company, you want to make sure they have established systems and processes in place so the business runs efficiently.

There are many, many questions you can ask, among them:

- What kinds of systems, processes and manuals do they have in place?
- Do they use a property management software? What kind?
- How long have they been in business?
- How many clients/landlords do they currently have?
- Is the company licensed (if your state requires that)?
- How many people does the company employ?
- Is the property maintenance work done in-house?
- How many third-party home repair vendors do they have on their Rolodex? (Plumbers, electricians, HVAC, etc.)
- How do they market their properties for rent?
- What is the average cost to turn a property?

- How long does it take them to get a property tenanted?
- How many properties do they currently manage?
- What is their average vacancy rate?
- What types of asset classes do they manage?
- What fees do they charge? Are they reasonable compared to other companies?
- Is there a separate trust account for collecting the rent deposits?
- Are they responsive to clients (investors) and tenants?
- Do they have an emergency hotline?
- And what are the biggest "pain points" in their business right now?

All of these questions are ultimately important to ask. And then depending on the answers, you'll be able to decide whether this particular property management company is one that you would be interested in bringing on board to assist you with managing your property or properties.

They all have different structures and ways of doing business, just like any other company in any other industry. It all comes down to your preference and what/who you feel most comfortable with.

The most important consideration, in my opinion, is what their longtime clients have to say about them. Reviews are extremely powerful.

Make sure to spend time reading these in detail on Google, Facebook, Better Business Bureau, Yelp and other review sites. When there are complaints (and there will be a ton, as such is the property management industry in general), how does the property management company reply? If there is a problem, do they offer a solution?

Look especially at the reviews from landlords. What you're going to find is most of the complaints will come from the tenants, which is normal, because it's very hard to win when you're dealing with tenants and toilets. But if the actual landlords are posting good comments and good reviews, then that in my opinion is more powerful than any tenant complaint.

Finally, if you genuinely want to be a passive investor, I recommend working with a true turnkey operator. As I said previously, that means the turkey provider has its own property management company in-house.

Lessons Learned the Hard Way

At Ohio Cashflow, we learned very early in the game how important that is. Not only is it simply more efficient, but it's also the best way of ensuring your investors' interest is always No. 1. That has always been our priority, even when we were just starting out and learning property management best practices ourselves. We have never compromised and never will, even though we had some disastrous times in the beginning.

We made every mistake known to mankind when we started our property management company. First, because we didn't know any better, we were managing unlicensed, which is a big, big no-no. Especially in Ohio. If you do not have a licensed broker when you are managing properties, you can get into a whole world of trouble, and the fines are absolutely ridiculous. Thank goodness, we quickly woke up and smelled the roses and we realized we needed a licensed broker on staff. So we hired one, but then, our licensed broker died (I'm not kidding), so we had to scramble to find a replacement. We also were not using any property management software; we were simply calculating everything with freaking pen and paper, which is also a big no-no. And if that weren't enough, we didn't have a separate trust account for collecting all of the deposits, which can mean jail time. You name it, we made all of the mistakes known to mankind when it comes to property management. I could go on, but that's enough to paint you a picture of just how screwed up we were in the beginning.

But one thing that we always did correctly, and that was no matter how many times we messed up, no matter how many mistakes we made, no matter what happened, we would always look after our investors and tenants.

We know that no one is going to look after investors as much as we do. We want them to do well with their investments. We want them to buy more properties. And with our property management in-house and now doing all the right things, we can go above and beyond to keep management fees affordable so they can get the highest possible return on investment. They're happy, we're happy. Investors buy more properties, we make more sales, the investors earn more cashflow ,and everybody grows and prospers. A true win/win for all.

But again I caution you: Not all turnkey companies operate like this. Not all property management companies have your best interests at heart. Make sure you do your extreme due diligence when choosing who to work with, so you don't end up making a bad deal with the Devil.

"Don't trip over dollars to pick up pennies."
— Unknown

Chapter 21

ALL ROADS LEAD TO ROME (OR BOATS TO THE BAHAMAS)

You might be surprised to learn that one of the most powerful tools upon which your success depends are "to-do" lists. In fact, I think writing things down—and keeping those notes for future reference— is extremely important, if not one of *the* most important things that you need to do daily. If you don't write things down, the likelihood of remembering it all is slim to none. All those notes and lists are critical to getting you from here to there, from where you are today to where you ultimately want to be.

Let me give you an example. Years ago, I started writing down my "big picture" goals and reverse-engineering and breaking down those goals into smaller, achievable targets—for example on a monthly, quarterly, half-yearly and annual basis.

Today, it absolutely amazes me how I can look back to those pieces of paper—which were literally written on napkins or scraps—and find myself thinking, "Wow; I completely nailed those goals in 2014, 2015 (or whatever year it may be)." When you write things down and review them regularly, it truly becomes a part of you. It's like your subconscious mind works on those goals until they come to fruition. I call it the "Miracle of Goal Writing." You dream your thoughts into reality.

You have to write things down because that's how they become something that you live and breathe. The saying, "What the mind can perceive, it can achieve," is very true. There is nothing in this world that you can't have. If you believe in it, and you want it that badly, you can achieve it. You will attain that goal. Trust me. I have, and I don't know of many that are "less qualified" or bigger bums than me. If I can do it, so can you, mate.

Live it, Breathe it, Accomplish it!

The law of attraction also speaks to this belief. If you make your whole life revolve around one particular thing, whatever your goal may be, and if you live it and you breathe it, and it haunts you day and night, you will have no other choice but to work hard enough to make it a reality. It's amazing how it happens, but it just does.

I spend September and October of every year thinking about my goals and I'll sporadically review them throughout the rest of the year (mostly when I fly somewhere and I have time to kill on the plane). Just recently I finished writing my goals down for two years from now. How about that? Things and circumstances do change so you constantly need to keep adding, removing and tweaking. But the principle stays the same. Those future goals have already become a part of me just because it's an ongoing process of adding, removing, tweaking, wishing, wanting, desiring. And working. Eventually they happen, like a miracle. Subconsciously, I think, we work toward the goals because they really have become a part of us. I'm telling you, mates, it's the "Miracle of Goal Writing." You have to do it. *Please…*

The Power of Four

I actually have four types of to-do lists: Urgent, Pertinent, Calendar and Notepad. Here's how I use them:

- **Urgent**: I have a whiteboard right behind me for the urgent list. I call this my do-or-die list. It is where I put things that are most important and need to happen quickly. I review/update it every day.

- **Pertinent**: A second whiteboard on the wall to my left is for goals on a weekly and monthly timeline, along with a variety of other performance metrics and stats. This keeps them always in my line of sight. When I have meetings with my team or whoever pops into my office, the whiteboards are part of our discussion focus. I also sometimes like to "throw" random stuff on the whiteboard just to have a record of it.

- **Calendar**: I keep my daily calendar on my laptop and phone, and it's where all the nitty-gritty happens: Meetings, phone calls, appointments and other tasks, scheduled in half-hour increments. I share this calendar with my team, as they schedule a lot of stuff in there for me also.

- **Notepad**: This notepad usually has about 20–30 rotating things on it, and I add items and cross them off when I've accomplished them. There is no urgency or anything specific with the notepad. It could be random thoughts or something that I need to get done. It's also for the "feel-good factor." I like crossing stuff off the list as things are completed.

Additional Tools I Use

Those aren't the only tools I use. I also keep tasks in Podio and Asana, project management and collaboration software (Podio also acts as a CRM); they can be daily, weekly, monthly or even yearly. I use Slack, a file-, message- and video-sharing application, to send my team and myself messages about ideas I don't want to forget. Then there is Google Sheets, which is awesome for tracking metrics and stats, and Trello, which is like an assembly-line platform for tech projects. And finally, I have what I call my little Magic Black Book, or my million-dollar book. This is where I record any ideas of significance, even the ones that seem crazy at the time. The Magic Black Book is never more than five feet away from me. (Touching my Black Book gets you in a lot of trouble!)

It may sound confusing, overwhelming and inefficient. To a certain level, I would agree. The thing is: It works. It really just comes down to "whatever floats your boat." You can use my methods as a guide, but ultimately you need to decide how you want to go about your to-do lists. My method has worked for me and hopefully you find one that can work for you. Peace! This is what I mean by living and breathing your goals; you need them to be ever-present. You need to have them all around you. You need direction, and that direction is provided with these lists. They make up your roadmap. They will get you where you need to be. I know it seems excessive, but the "maze" of lists I showed you has enabled me to be where I am today.

Of course, none of this works if you don't "work" or have a solid end goal. We've touched on this earlier, but let's review more deeply how it would translate to putting your own lists together.

Everything Revolves Around Your End Goal

The end goal is a monetary equivalent, a certain amount of money which, when invested at a certain rate, will produce a certain amount of cash flow. Every transaction (property purchase) that you conduct has to get you a step closer toward achieving that end goal. All of your actions on a daily basis have to be in tune with that end-goal vision and also have to get you a step closer to achieving your end goal. Any action that contradicts that vision (like starting another venture and chasing the "shiny object" when the "shiny object" wouldn't get you closer to your desired end goal) will just slow you down in getting to where you really want to be. That's *The Raw Truth.*

Once you have your end goal set, you have to reverse-engineer, working backward to break that goal down into pieces. We've previously used the example of having $1.2 million in net wealth (free and clear) producing 10 percent net cash flow in 10 years' time, which will be $120,000 a year. If I break this into smaller increments, here's what they are (approximately):

- In five years, I need to be at $600,000, so…
- In three years, I need to be at $360,000, so…
- In one year, I need to be at $120,000, so…
- Every quarter I need to retain $30,000, so…
- Every month, I need to retain $10,000 or so…
- Every week, I need to retain about $2,310, so…
- Every day, I need to be retaining about $330.

Suddenly, things get clearer and the mountain seems smaller, right? Now that you've broken down the numbers, you have to break down the efforts needed to achieve the numbers. After selecting an investment strategy, you reverse-engineer your actions the same way you did with the money. It might look something like this (remember, you're breaking the goal into smaller and smaller pieces until you get to your daily tasks):

- How many properties do you need to flip? To buy and hold? To wholesale?

- How much are those properties going to cost? And where will you find them?
- How much do you need in order to purchase the first property and what team do you need in place?
- How are you going to make that amount of money and how will you find the team?
- Where can you get a job to earn that money or even a second job to earn faster?
- Where can you buy a computer so that you can create your resume and start researching real estate markets along with doing the real estate license training?
- How much will the computer cost? And where is the closest library?
- Who will help you create your resume?
- How are you going to make the money to buy that computer?
- Can you bum some change from a mate to buy a computer?

This is what I am talking about. You simply reverse-engineer all the way back to the current day and then you can put together your various to-do lists. Here is an example based on the above: It's a detailed thought process. But that is how you have to be, never skipping a beat. Because the big picture and vision are never going to fall into place unless you do the small things consistently and daily.

That's what I'm best known for: Doing the small things on a consistent basis. There is no talent necessarily associated with it; it's just pure, hard work. Stay consistent with the hours you commit, with the emails you send, the phone calls you make, the videos you do, the hands you shake, the offers you submit. They say that half of the work is done just by showing up. I can attest to this being true. No matter how you feel or what is going on in your personal life, wake up and show up every day.

Do yourself a favor and start putting your lists together *today*.

Here are some questions to ask yourself to get you started:

- Where do you want to be in five years? 10 years from now?
- How much money do you want to be making? Passively?
- How are you going to get there?
- What strategy should you be using to make that money?
- How and where can you learn that strategy?
- What basic skills do you need to have?
- If you don't have those skills, where can you get them?
- Do you need a mentor to help you?
- Why are you doing all of this?
- Who are you doing this for?
- Are you prepared to do whatever it takes to achieve your goals?

Every ounce of your being and everything you do need to complement your bigger picture and vision. That's the only way to make your dream become reality.

Also, never forget that doing the small things on a consistent basis is what enables the big things to fall into place. It's *The Raw Truth*.

I believe in you and want you to succeed.

Your time is now. Are you ready to get started on your own path from here to there?

> *"Success is a journey, not a destination.*
> *The doing is often more important than the outcome."*
> — Arthur Ashe

Chapter 22

GIVE IT YOUR ALL, AND THEN GIVE IT ALL AWAY

I was at the lowest point of my life. My mom had been diagnosed with cancer. I had sour business relationships and was more than $1 million in debt. (Mind you, I had already been investing in real estate for a few years at this point.) I owed money on credit cards and everywhere you could possibly imagine. I fractured my left wrist and I couldn't afford to fix it. It was literally fractured for a year. To make matters even worse, I also recently had gotten out of a long-term relationship. I felt like the whole world was caving in.

And then my grandma, Milka, the love of my life, passed away. (My mum, Nancy, and grandma were the only two women who could put up with a younger, hyperactive Engelo.) Everyone else rejected me as a child.

I remember slumping to the ground and weeping heavily, and then I just felt something flash through my entire body. To this day, it's hard to explain exactly what it was. I guess it was the realization that there was no way I could get any lower. This was it. This was rock-bottom. It couldn't get any worse.

It was a life-changing moment. Right there and then, even though I didn't know it, is when I found my purpose and my "why" in life.

I remember picking myself back up and going down to my cramped, rathole little office in the hallway of a co-working space. I spent the next nine months eating peanut butter sandwiches and drinking $1 gas station coffee just to survive, but I hustled every single day from dawn to dusk.

It wasn't just me, though. The sexy, smart and super successful Dominique (the unsung hero of this book and our entrepreneurial journey) was by my side the whole time. We committed to "the numbers." Nine months later, we established a relationship with a "sales channel." In time we sold 22 properties, which enabled us to clear the majority of my debt, fix my wrist, help my mum, settle the sour business relationships and get going with Ohio Cashflow, our bread-and-butter company and the means to our end-goal plans.

Those nine months were trying times, full of soul-searching and self-questioning, along with a bunch of disgusting B.S. thrown at me by *everyone*. It enabled me to find the meaning and "why" in what I'm doing. It's not about my own ego. It's not about money. It's about something bigger and better than that.

You Must Help Yourself First

First of all, I had to help myself, because if I can help myself and I'm in good standing, I can help those around me. (Remember, on airplanes they require that you put on your own oxygen mask first.)

What drives me, what inspires me, what pushes me every single day is the opportunity to provide a better life for my loved ones (family and friends), for people who are associated with my companies (employees and other folks), for the investors who have trusted us with their hard-earned money (thank you to all for your trust and belief), and then for something that is bigger and better than one could imagine: A legacy. When everything is said and done and I am no more, I want whatever I leave behind to continue helping hundreds of thousands, if not millions, of people across the world. It's *The Raw Truth*.

Perhaps I'll start the Rumora Institute for Cancer Research, or the Rumora Institute for Anxiety. (I have suffered from anxiety and panic attacks since longer than I can remember.) Whatever it may be, my purpose and "why" in life is to give it my all.

Once I achieve greatness and unlimited amounts of money, I want to give it all away. I personally can't wait for the day when I can stop calculating financial targets, and instead start counting how many people I have helped and how many lives I have changed. As corny as it all might sound, it truly is what's in my heart and soul.

Finding your purpose and your "why" in life is the most powerful thing that can ever happen to you. (For me, it was the moment my grandma died.) When you do find it, you'll feel like Superman or Wonder Woman. You'll have no fear. You'll endure no hunger. You'll feel no pain. All you will feel is a sheer drive, passion and determination to succeed in your undertaking. You will feel unstoppable. And when you feel unstoppable, you can create something bigger and better than you could ever imagine. Or that anyone else could have ever imagined.

Be Passionate About What You Do

When your alarm goes off in the morning, do you ever hit the snooze button? Sure, everyone does. But why do you? If you are going to your 9-to-5 to make money, you shouldn't hit snooze, right? If that job that you "love so dearly" or that money you earn was a strong enough factor, you wouldn't. You would get up immediately (like a bee stung your behind) and go. But instead, you grab a few extra minutes in bed and get to work at 9:15 a.m. This is a prime example of how making money itself is not a strong enough purpose or "why."

How about your own personal ego? Can your own personal ego or "yourself" be your purpose in life? Not really. (Don't get me wrong; I absolutely love to see my face on TV, magazines and everywhere else, because I suffer from the complex of never having become the huge professional soccer player that I always wanted to be.) But ego is not enough on its own to motivate me—or you. Sometimes you give up on yourself.

Have you ever said, "I'm going to go to the gym and lose weight" or get super-fit? Yes, I'll bet you have. Did you still eat those pesky carbs/sugars or skip the gym because you were too tired? Yes, you did. You didn't honor your strict diet plan or training regimen.

So doing it for you and your personal ego and your looks just don't add up to being a strong enough purpose and "why" to push you through the tough times (those tough times will break you unless you have your purpose and "why" really figured out).

But now let me ask you this. If a loved one slipped and was about to fall to his or her death off a cliff, but you caught them in the last millisecond, would you let go? No, you wouldn't. You would hang on forever, even if it was hanging by your last artery. You would never let go even if it meant falling with or before just to save them.

Now that's a strong enough purpose and will to even sacrifice yourself if you have to. It's not about you, and it's not about your money; it's about your family. That's a much bigger purpose and a far greater "why" than your ego or your checkbook.

Even though I told you to tell your family to screw off, in my opinion, your purpose needs to revolve around your loved ones. In one way or another, it needs to revolve around other people. Other people whom you can't let down no matter what. Or even a cause. Far greater than you, me or anyone. Something that never dies and can live on forever serving and helping others.

How Do You Find Your Purpose?

I get asked all the time about how to find your "why," but I don't know the answer to that question, I'm sorry. But I can give you my theory on what I believe molded me to find mine. I am a big believer that your network is your net worth and that no matter who they are or what they do, you should stop and listen, if only for a minute.

The more people you speak with on a daily basis and the more questions you ask, the more your mind will expand, the more you will learn, the more you will know and the better you will become. You just might get inspired by something that these individuals have to say about their past, present or future. That inspiration will help you search within yourself and find why you exist, why it is that you are on this planet and what it is that you are meant to be doing.

Talk to as many people as you possibly can and listen to their stories. Ask them why they do what they do. Just think about how many people you drive or pass by every day who do not know why they live their lives. Maybe that's you, also. They don't know why they get out of bed every morning. They have no meaning. They go to their 9-to-5 jobs like zombies, to pay off a mortgage and can't wait for the weekend to spank the rest and get hammered drunk. There is no substance to it. There is no bigger picture. There is no vision. There is no legacy there. *There is no purpose.* There is more to life than that, and you, I and everyone else need to be on a mission to find it. It's called "happiness."

Adding another $1,000 or $10,000 or $100,000 to your net wealth will not make you any happier or more fulfilled either. One of my favorite quotes is from life coach Tony Robbins: "Success without fulfillment is the ultimate failure."

I know a lot of people out there who are adding millions of dollars to their account, but it doesn't make them happy, and it doesn't make them fulfilled. They are miserable jerks that nobody likes. Even I don't yet have everything completely figured out and am still on a mission to find true happiness. It's not easy, but I won't stop searching and neither should you.

More money will not change who you are; it will magnify who you already are. If you're a good person, it will allow you to be a better person and do even more good. If you're a worthless piece of garbage, you're going to be an even bigger one. Take a long, hard look at yourself in the mirror. What do you see? Are you happy? Who are you? What do you really want?

Ultimately, you need to find fulfillment in what you do. There's nothing better. Personally, I like giving much more than I do receiving (I want to be remembered as the King of Hearts and not Diamonds). Of course, I am going to have whatever my heart desires in regard to materialistic pleasures, and I want to achieve all of my goals and bucket list items. And rightly so. Nothing was ever handed to me on a silver platter, and I've worked my butt off (and still do) for all of it. But at the end of the day, when I give something of value to someone, the smile on their face really touches my heart, and I will carry that with me forever. I will never forget that as long as I live.

Those are the types of memories that I want to be building and cherishing. So that is why most of what I do, this book that you're reading, pretty much anything else outside of my core business model, is all for charitable purposes.

That is my fulfillment, that is my "why," and that is my purpose.

Mates, I hope this book has inspired and motivated you. Even kicked you up the backside if you needed it. Although most of the content is rude, raw and "in your face," I still hope that you found it useful and that it will help you on your real estate investment journey. Against all odds, *I made it* and I know that you can, too. Thanks for reading and I wish you all the love, health and happiness that you desire.

Yours truly,
Engelo Rumora
#RealEstateDingo
"I will give it my all and will give it all away."

"When I was 5 years old, my mother told me that happiness was the key to life. When I went to school, they asked me what I wanted to be when I grew up. I wrote down 'Happy.' They told me that I didn't understand the assignment, and I told them that they didn't understand life."
— John Lennon

FOR EVERYONE WHO WANTS TO CONTINUE BEING A "LAZY A-HOLE," I CAN HELP!

VISIT ENGELORUMORA.COM TO FIND OUT MORE.

ACKNOWLEDGMENTS

Ciao a tutti,
Belli e brutti

First of all, I want to thank all of the readers. I'd also like to sincerely apologize if I have offended you in any way or if you didn't find this book useful. Those who know me well can vouch that there is a good soul underneath all of the S#%@ talk. My hope was that you could at least have one major takeaway with which you could make your real estate investing better.

I'm forever grateful to these five people as they have been the biggest influences in my life: Mum for her sacrifice. Dad for his integrity. Dominique for always caring. Norbert for his positivity, and Milka for her never-ending love. A big thanks to Linda for her amazing work with this book. You have always guessed my voice perfectly in all of your writing. Isaac, for your wisdom and friendship. We just have so much in common. Lonna Mangus, for being hard-working and loyal to our various companies. And Jaelynn Zoe for being gorgeous, smart, good and for putting up with her Big Papino.

All of my family: Patricia, Rocco, Raphaella, Mladen, Jasna, Eva, Tonini, Deda, Darko, Renee, John, Brie (sorry if I missed anyone).

Jim and Chris Howard from Morgan James, for giving such a controversial/provocative figure like me a chance.

For everyone from my past, present and future. For everyone who knows me, hates me and loves me. I'm grateful for the experience and also apologetic at the same time. I'm trying to love you all and to be grateful to you all, no matter what.

There are probably so many other people who slipped my mind while writing this who deserve a mention. Just know that you do cross my thoughts even though your name isn't mentioned above. I am grateful to you.

That's it for now, and never forget that at the end of the day, nothing really matters.

ABOUT THE AUTHOR

Engelo Rumora, a.k.a. "the Real Estate Dingo," quit school at the age of 14 and played professional soccer at the age of 18. From there, he began to invest in real estate. He now owns real estate all over the world and has bought, renovated and sold over 1,000 properties. He runs Ohio Cashflow, among the top turnkey real estate investment companies in the country (Inc. 5000 2017 & 2018). He is also known for giving houses away to people in need and his crazy videos on YouTube. His mission in life is to be remembered as someone who gave it his all and gave it all away.